THE BRITANNICA GUIDE TO
FOOTBALL

THE WORLD OF SPORTS

THE BRITANNICA GUIDE TO
FOOTBALL

EDITED BY ADAM AUGUSTYN, ASSISTANT EDITOR
AND ASSISTANT MANAGER, SPORTS

Britannica
Educational Publishing

IN ASSOCIATION WITH

ROSEN
EDUCATIONAL SERVICES

Published in 2011 by Britannica Educational Publishing
(a trademark of Encyclopædia Britannica, Inc.)
in association with Rosen Educational Services, LLC
29 East 21st Street, New York, NY 10010.

First Edition

Britannica Educational Publishing
Michael I. Levy: Executive Editor
J.E. Luebering: Senior Manager
Marilyn L. Barton: Senior Coordinator, Production Control
Steven Bosco: Director, Editorial Technologies
Lisa S. Braucher: Senior Producer and Data Editor
Yvette Charboneau: Senior Copy Editor
Kathy Nakamura: Manager, Media Acquisition
Adam Augustyn: Assistant Manager, Encyclopedia Britannica

Rosen Educational Services
Jeanne Nagle: Senior Editor
Nelson Sá: Art Director
Cindy Reiman: Photography Manager
Karen Huang: Photo Researcher
Matthew Cauli: Designer, Cover Design
Introduction by Adam Augustyn

Library of Congress Cataloging-in-Publication Data

The Britannica guide to football / edited by Adam Augustyn.
    p. cm. — (The world of sports)
"In association with Britannica Educational Publishing, Rosen Educational Services."
Includes bibliographical references and index.
ISBN 978-1-61530-524-7 (library binding)
1. Football. I. Augustyn, Adam, 1979- II. Britannica Educational Publishing.
GV951.B85 2012
796.332—dc22

                                                                    2011005996

Manufactured in the United States of America

Cover, pp. x-xi, 1, 20, 45, 55, 134, 165, 201, 230, 231, 243, 245, 247, back cover Shutterstock.
com; background image on pp. v, vi, vii, viii, ix ©www.istockphoto.com/David Lee; interior
background image (football) ©www.istockphoto.com/Nick M. Do; interior background image
(field) ©www.istockphoto.com/Mark Herreid

CONTENTS

3

7

22

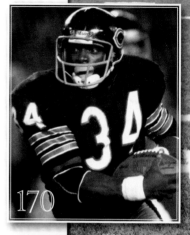

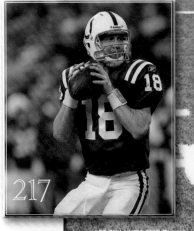

INTRODUCTION

Gridiron football has saturated modern American culture more than any other sport. Youngsters play the game early and often in the United States, whether it's part of an organized youth league (often Pee Wee or Pop Warner football), at the junior high and high school levels, or merely a pickup game played on a vacant stretch of land. Unrivaled in its appeal to a television audience, watching college football and the fantastically popular professional National Football League (NFL) is a weekly autumn ritual for a vast—and continuously growing—audience.

The sport traces its roots to soccer and rugby. Football originated in 19th-century American universities, where students organized informal, soccer-style contests on various campuses. The first intercollegiate football game was played in 1869 between what are now known as Princeton University and Rutgers, the State University of New Jersey. The soccer-style game spread throughout colleges in the Northeast, with the notable exception of Harvard University, where a rugby-soccer hybrid known as the "Boston Game" was played. The two styles of football existed side-by-side until 1876, when four Northeast universities formed the Intercollegiate Football Association and based their game on rugby rules.

The rugby style of play began to transform in what is now recognized as gridiron football primarily through the efforts of Walter Camp, the "Father of American Football." As a member of the game's early rules committee, Camp initiated the change, in 1880, from a rugby scrummage for determining possession of the ball, which kept the ball moving back and forth between the two opposing sides, to a scrimmage, which awarded the ball to one of the two teams for a prolonged period in order to increase scoring opportunities. His other landmark innovation came two years later when, in an effort to stop the frustrating strategy of simply holding the ball for the duration of a game, he proposed that a team must advance the ball 5 yards or move back 10 in three plays, or else surrender possession. These two important modifications opened up the game, and speed became as important a skill for football players to possess as strength. Camp introduced a number of other features of the modern game, including position names, having 11 players on a side, and the legalization of tackling below the waist. Over time, the sport continued to change and came to resemble something completely distinct from rugby by the turn of the 20th century.

As football grew, a greater number of Americans began to become alarmed by the violence in the young game. In 1905 alone, 18 individuals died from football injuries, which prompted U.S. Pres. Theodore Roosevelt to call on university representatives to reform the game. The reform movement resulted in the founding of the Intercollegiate Athletic Association, which later grew into the National

Collegiate Athletic Association (NCAA), the administrative body of all college athletics. In an effort to stop the dangerous "mass plays"—the strategy of massing offensive players on a single point of the defense that was the source of many of the injuries at the time—the NCAA increased the yardage needed for a first down to 10 and legalized the forward pass. These changes lessened football-related deaths, but it was only with additional rule changes over the years and the advent of safety equipment, namely helmets, that the sport began to become truly accepted by the public at large.

College football was the dominant form of the game through the early years of the 20th century. Beginning in 1902, an unofficial national collegiate champion was decided in a game known as the Rose Bowl, an incredibly lucrative venture that inspired a proliferation of regional bowl games, many of which were still being played into the 21st century. By the 1920s college football was one of the most popular sports in the U.S., with radio networks and newsreels dedicating a significant amount of their time to coverage of the sport and total attendance at college games exceeding 10 million annually.

As collegiate football grew in prominence it expanded well beyond its original narrow Northeast base. Today it has been embraced by all parts of the U.S., particularly in the Southeast and Midwest. From the University of Washington to the University of Miami (Fla.), popular college football powerhouses can now be found in nearly every corner of America.

The emergence of college football on the national sporting scene was due in large part to the thrilling play of the University of Illinois' Red Grange, a halfback who captivated America with his signature long touchdown runs. Arguably his most significant impact on the sport came when he controversially dropped out of Illinois in

1925 and signed with the professional Chicago Bears of the nascent NFL. Grange's move lent legitimacy to the NFL, which up until that point had long been considered disreputable by the general public. The move also symbolically marked the beginning of a torch-passing from college football to the professional game as the more popular version of the sport, a shift that came about in the following decades.

The NFL was founded in 1920 as the American Professional Football Association (the name was changed two years later) and comprised teams primarily based in Midwestern towns. The small population bases of the young league limited its broader nationwide appeal until, in 1933, the NFL was reorganized into two five-team divisions of teams based in large cities. The only exception was the Green Bay Packers, who established themselves as one of the most successful—and profitable—professional teams of the 1930s, allowing them to thrive in the new NFL. On the field, the game became even more fan-friendly during this decade, which saw the emergence of the forward pass—a tactic that had been used only sparingly since it was legalized—as a vital offensive weapon. Quarterback Sammy Baugh of the Washington Redskins was a key figure in this development of the game.

Over time, the NFL grew prosperous enough to inspire a number of short-lived competitors to form. One rival league, the All-America Football Conference (AAFC), was a serious enough challenger to merit the absorption of three of its franchises—including the Cleveland Browns and San Francisco 49ers—into the NFL in 1950.

Professional football fully came into its own in 1958. That year's NFL championship matched the New York Giants against the Johnny Unitas–led Baltimore Colts, with the game going into sudden-death overtime. The Colts were the eventual victors, besting the Giants

23–17 on a one-yard touchdown run by Alan Ameche. That contest became known as "The Greatest Game Ever Played," not just because of its dramatic finish but because it was one of the first professional football games to truly capture the country's attention through a live national television broadcast. What followed was a veritable golden age of professional football in the U.S. Stars of the 1960s — such as running backs Jim Brown and Gale Sayers, linebacker Dick Butkus, and defensive end Deacon Jones — became some of the most iconic figures in the history of the game, due in no small part to the unprecedented familiarity the public had with this era of players.

As the NFL grew more prominent, a rival league emerged that would forever change the face of pro football. The American Football league (AFL) was founded in 1960, with three of the league's eight teams in direct competition with NFL franchises. The young league raided the NFL and lured away some of its best talent. The AFL also won the hearts of many football fans courtesy of the high-scoring aerial attack employed by most of the league's teams. The AFL was such a threat that the NFL agreed to a merger of the two associations in 1966, which was completed in 1970.

In the interim, the two leagues began playing an annual championship game in January 1967, which was renamed the Super Bowl in 1969. The NFL's Green Bay Packers handily won the first two titles, solidifying the common perception that the AFL was, while extremely popular, an inferior league. This belief was upended at Super Bowl III in 1969, when the AFL's New York Jets — led by cocky quarterback Joe Namath, who had guaranteed victory before the game — upset the heavily favored NFL Baltimore Colts. Super Bowl III not only showed that the AFL teams could compete with the NFL in the post-merger league, it also served to announce the arrival of the media-savvy Namath, who himself was a precursor for the star-driven showmanship that would soon come to define the league.

The expanded NFL continued to make its mark on the American sporting scene in the 1970s as the Dallas Cowboys, Oakland Raiders, and Pittsburgh Steelers variously dominated the game and established iconic "football brands" ("America's Team," "the Silver and Black," "the Steel Curtain") that persist to the present day. But the most notable single team of the decade was the 1972 Miami Dolphins, who went 17–0 to become the first— and, to date, only—NFL team to finish a season (including postseason play) without a loss.

The 1980s saw the emergence of a great number of standout quarterbacks who propelled the sport to unparalleled heights. Dan Marino of the Miami Dolphins rewrote the record book while the Denver Broncos' John Elway established a reputation as one of the greatest clutch performers in any sport. The greatest quarterback of this era—and, to many observers, the greatest of any era—was Joe Montana of the San Francisco 49ers. Montana guided the 49ers to four titles in the '80s. His famed rapport with wide receiver Jerry Rice made for one of the most celebrated passing duos in NFL history.

The dawning of a new millennium has seen the proliferation of satellite television and the Internet, which have expanded football's reach to every corner of the globe. The Super Bowl annually draws one of the largest international television audiences. Yet despite all this exposure, football has not gained the same degree of widespread popularity worldwide as certain other sports, such as baseball. An offshoot league, NFL Europe, proved to be a moderately successful venture but failed to ignite a passion for gridiron football in Europe. The league folded in 2007 after 15 seasons of play. The one country outside the U.S. that has taken to football is Canada. This is not surprising, considering that the country played a key role in the development of the game. McGill University in Montreal was one of the first North American universities to take up the sport, and it was McGill that introduced the rugby-style game to Harvard in 1874. The Canadian Football League (CFL), formed in 1956, has presented the Grey Cup trophy to the top Canadian football club for over a century.

Gridiron football is a game of contradictions. The same sport that, at its heart, is defined by the simple ethos of "find the ball, get the ball" is also, on a larger scale, an incredibly intricate and complex interplay of 22 players who move around the field like chess pieces. The game is both brutally physical and incredibly cerebral. The bone-rattling violence that has led many to call for a ban of the game over the years is balanced by the preternatural grace displayed by its greatest athletes. These contradictions are what make the sport appealing to a broad spectrum of fans in the melting pot that is America. As the U.S. populace continues to grow even more heterogeneous in the 21st century, football promises to remain one of the country's few enduring cultural touchstones.

CHAPTER 1

THE EARLY HISTORY
OF FOOTBALL

G ridiron football is a version of the sport of football (characterized by two people or teams attempting to kick, carry, throw, or otherwise propel a ball toward an opponent's goal) so named for the vertical yard lines marking the rectangular field. Gridiron football evolved from English rugby and soccer (association football). It differs from soccer chiefly in allowing players to touch, throw, and carry the ball with their hands, and it differs from rugby in allowing each side to control the ball in alternating possessions. The sport, played with 11 on each team, originated in the United States, where it was largely developed and eventually became the country's leading spectator sport. It quickly spread to Canada—where it evolved into a 12-man game—though it never achieved the great popularity and status of ice hockey there.

Gridiron football has not been taken up in the rest of the world to the same degree as other American sports such as basketball and baseball. Since the 1980s, however, primarily through the marketing efforts of the National Football League (NFL), teams and leagues have been established in Europe, and the game has achieved a degree of international popularity through television.

THE GAME EMERGES

Gridiron football was the creation of elite American universities, a fact that has shaped its distinctive role in American culture and life. After several decades of informal, student-organized games that were tolerated by faculty as an alternative to more destructive rowdiness, the first intercollegiate football game was played on Nov. 6, 1869, in New Brunswick, New Jersey, between in-state rivals Princeton and Rutgers according to rules adapted from those of the London Football Association. This soccer-style game became the dominant form as Columbia, Cornell, Yale, and a few other colleges in the Northeast took up the sport in the early 1870s.

In 1873 representatives from Princeton, Yale, and Rutgers met in New York City to found the Intercollegiate Football Association and to adopt a common code. Conspicuously missing was Harvard, the country's premier university, whose team insisted on playing the so-called "Boston Game," a cross between soccer and rugby. In May 1874, in the second of two matches with McGill University of Montreal (the first was played by the rules of the Boston Game), Harvard's players were introduced to the rugby game and immediately preferred it to their own. The following year, for Harvard's first football contest with Yale, representatives of the two schools agreed on "concessionary rules" that were chiefly Harvard's. When spectators (including Princeton students) as well as Yale players saw the advantages of the rugby style, the stage was set for a meeting in 1876 of representatives from Harvard, Yale, Princeton, and Columbia to form a new Intercollegiate Football Association based on rugby rules.

WALTER CAMP AND THE CREATION OF AMERICAN FOOTBALL

Harvard made the first breach in rugby rules. Rejecting the traditional manner of putting the ball in play—players from both teams massed about the ball in a "scrummage,"

Walter Camp is largely responsible for the advent of gridiron football in America. Hulton Archive/Getty Images

or "scrum," trying to kick it forward through the mass of players—Harvard opted for "heeling it out," or kicking the ball backward to a teammate. The further transformation of English rugby into American football came chiefly through the efforts of Walter Camp, who even during his lifetime was known as the "Father of American Football."

As an undergraduate and then a medical student at Yale, Camp played football from 1876 through 1881, but— more important—beginning in 1878, he dominated the rules committee for nearly three crucial decades. Two of Camp's revisions in particular effectively created the gridiron game. The first, in 1880, further refined Harvard's initial innovation, abolishing the scrummage altogether in favour of a scrimmage, which awarded possession of the ball to one of the two teams. It was then put in play by heeling it out. (Snapping the ball with the hand became legal in 1890, though snapping with the foot continued as an option until 1913.)

The second crucial rule change was necessitated by the first. Camp's more orderly manner of initiating play did not require the team in possession of the ball to give it up. After Princeton simply held the ball for an entire half in its 1880 and 1881 contests with Yale, both games ending in scoreless ties that bored spectators as much as they frustrated Yale's players, Camp proposed a rule that a team must advance the ball 5 yards or lose 10 in three downs (plays), or it would be obliged to surrender the ball to the other side.

Camp also was responsible for having 11 players on a side, for devising a new scoring system in 1883 with two points for a touchdown, four points for the goal after a touchdown, and five points for a field goal (a field goal became worth three points in 1909, a touchdown six points in 1912), for naming the positions (centre, guard, tackle, end, quarterback, halfback, fullback), for

WALTER CAMP

(b. April 7, 1859, New Britain, Conn., U.S.—d. March 14, 1925, New York, N.Y.)

Although he is best known for having selected the earliest All-America teams in American college football, Walter Camp more importantly played a leading role in developing the American game as distinct from rugby football.

At Yale, Camp played halfback, served as team captain (at that time equivalent to head coach), and became a member of the Intercollegiate Football Association. This ruling body accepted a wide variety of innovations proposed by Camp that became fundamental building blocks of the game. Although he was an executive of a watch-manufacturing firm from 1883, Camp coached the Yale football team from 1888 through 1892, his teams winning 67 games while losing only two.

From 1889 through 1897, Camp and Caspar Whitney collaborated in choosing the annual All-America football team, an idea that seems to have originated with Whitney. From 1898 through 1924, the teams were announced in the magazine *Collier's* under the name of Camp alone. Upon his death he was succeeded as All-America selector by the noted sportswriter Grantland Rice. In 1951 he was in the first class to be inducted into the College Football Hall of Fame.

marking the field with stripes, and for proposing several other innovations. But it was those two simple rules adopted in 1880 and 1882 that most fundamentally created American football.

After the crucial rule changes, the play of the game was relatively open, featuring long runs and numerous lateral passes, as in rugby. In 1888 Camp proposed that tackling below the waist be legalized, in order to offset the advantage of speedy backs streaking around the ends. The new rule resulted in the rise of mass plays, an offensive strategy that massed players on a single point of the defense, most famously in Harvard's "flying wedge" in 1892. This style of play proved so brutal that the game was nearly abolished in the 1890s and early 1900s.

MANAGING THE VIOLENCE OF THE GAME

The spirit of early football can be glimpsed in the introduction of a rule in 1894 that banned projecting nails or iron plates in shoes and any metal substance on the player's person. Rules establishing boundaries between permissible and impermissible violence have been continually revised over the years, sometimes in response to periods of heightened concern over deaths and injuries (in the early 1930s as well as the 1890s, for example). To ensure greater safety, the number of officials grew from two in 1873 to seven by 1983.

Over time, improvements in equipment also provided more safeguards against serious injuries. In the 1890s players' only protection against blows to the head came from their own long hair and leather nose guards. The first headgear, in 1896, consisted simply of three leather straps. It evolved into close-fitting leather caps with ear flaps. The suspension helmet, which used straps to create space between the helmet shell and the head of the wearer, was introduced in 1917. However, helmets were not required in college football until 1939 (1943 for the NFL). Improved equipment sometimes increased rather than curtailed the game's dangers. The plastic helmet, introduced in 1939, became a potentially lethal weapon, eventually requiring rules against "spearing"—using the head to initiate contact.

EXPANSION AND REFORM

In 1879 the University of Michigan and Racine College of Wisconsin inaugurated football in the Midwest.

Leather helmets, introduced in the early 1900s, did not provide as much protection as today's plastic headgear, but they were a step up from the equipment used prior to that. Archive Photos/Getty Images

Michigan under Fielding Yost in 1901–05 and the University of Chicago under Amos Alonzo Stagg in 1905–09 emerged as major powers. The game also spread throughout the rest of the country by the 1890s, though the Big Three—Harvard, Yale, and Princeton—continued to dominate the collegiate football world into the 1920s. Ever mindful of their superiority to the latecomers, the three (joined by the University of Pennsylvania to create briefly a Big Four) formed the Intercollegiate Rules Committee in 1894, separate from the Intercollegiate Football Association. In 1895 in the Midwest, colleges dissatisfied with this divided leadership asserted their independence by forming what became the Western (now the Big Ten) Conference. The game also spread to the South and West, though conferences were not formed until later in those regions.

The brutality of mass play also spread through the nation. Over the course of the 1905 season, 18 young men died from football injuries. Concerned that football might be abolished altogether, President Theodore Roosevelt in October 1905 summoned representatives (including Camp) from Harvard, Yale, and Princeton to the White House, where he urged them to reform the game. On December 28 of that year representatives from 62 colleges and universities (not including the Big Three, who would continue for decades to balk at submitting to the will of "inferior" institutions) met in New York to form the Intercollegiate Athletic Association of the United States, which became the National Collegiate Athletic Association (NCAA) in 1910.

To reduce mass play, the group at its initial meeting increased the yardage required for a first down from 5 yards to 10 and legalized the forward pass, the final element in the creation of the game of American football. The founding of the NCAA effectively ended the period when the

AMOS ALONZO STAGG

(b. Aug. 16, 1862, West Orange, N.J., U.S.—d. March 17, 1965, Stockton, Calif.)

Amos Alonzo Stagg had the longest coaching career—71 years—in the history of the football. In 1943, at the age of 81, he was named college coach of the year, and he remained active in coaching until the age of 98. He is the only person selected for the College Football Hall of Fame as both a player and a coach. He was also important in the development of intercollegiate basketball.

As an end for Yale, where he was also an outstanding baseball pitcher, Stagg was chosen for Walter Camp's first All-America football team (1889). He then attended the International Young Men's Christian Association (YMCA) Training School, afterward Springfield (Mass.) College; there he both played and coached football and became one of the first enthusiasts of basketball, which was invented by James Naismith at the Springfield school in 1891. On Jan. 18, 1896, Stagg's University of Chicago team defeated the University of Iowa in the first intercollegiate basketball game with five players on each side.

During Stagg's 41-year tenure (1892–1932) as football coach at Chicago, the Maroons won six Western Conference (Big Ten) championships outright (1899, 1905, 1907, 1908, 1913, 1924) and tied for another (1922). They were undefeated and untied in two seasons (1905, 1913) and undefeated but tied at least once in two other years (1899, 1908). For his Chicago teams he devised the end-around play, the man in motion, the huddle (also credited to Bob Zuppke, coach at the University of Illinois), the shift (later employed with great success by Knute Rockne at the University of Notre Dame), and the dummy for tackling practice. After his enforced retirement from Chicago at the age of 70, he was head coach at the College (now University) of the Pacific, Stockton, Calif. (1933–46); advisory coach at Susquehanna University, Selinsgrove, Pa., under his son, head coach Amos Alonzo Stagg, Jr. (1947–52); and advisory coach at Stockton Junior College (1953–60).

Big Three (and Walter Camp personally) dictated rules of play to the rest of the football world. It also ended student involvement in controlling the game, though the question of who should rule college football—coaches, alumni and boosters, or college administrators—would continue to bedevil the NCAA throughout its history.

Brutality did not end with the revised rules of 1906. New crises prompted additional rule changes in 1910 (requiring seven men on the line of scrimmage) and 1912 (increasing the number of downs to gain 10 yards from three to four) to eliminate mass play. Nor did the forward pass immediately transform the game. The restrictive 1906 rules made passes riskier than fumbles, and it was only after several years of cautious experimentation that Notre Dame's upset of Army in 1913 highlighted the remarkable possibilities in the passing game. It would be another three decades, however—during which restrictive rules were gradually dropped and the circumference of the ball reduced to facilitate passing—before those possibilities could be fully realized.

SPORT AND SPECTACLE

This early period in American football was formative in another way as well. Beginning in 1876, the original Intercollegiate Football Association staged a championship game at the end of each season, on Thanksgiving Day, matching the two best teams from the previous year. Initially the game was played in Hoboken, New Jersey, but in 1880 it was shifted to New York City to make it easier for students from all the universities in the association to attend the game. The attendance for that first contest in New York was 5,000. By 1884 it had climbed to 15,000. Attendance rose to 25,000 by 1890 and 40,000 by 1893, the last Thanksgiving Day game to be played in the city.

By this time, accounts of the game in New York's major newspapers were taking up as much as three pages in an eight-page paper, and wire services carried reports to every corner of the country. By the 1890s an extracurricular activity at a handful of elite northeastern universities was becoming a spectator sport with a nationwide audience. College football became known for its bands and cheerleaders, pep rallies and bonfires, and homecoming dances and alumni reunions as much as for its athletic thrills. Pursuing the institution's educational mission while serving the public's desire for entertainment posed a dilemma with which college administrators struggled for more than a century. For some of the public, college football's association with institutions of higher education and immersion in college spirit imbued the game with a kind of amateur purity. For others, the colleges' profession of commitment to academic goals while commercializing their sports teams only smacked of hypocrisy.

COLLEGE FOOTBALL'S GOLDEN AGE

After World War I had put the game temporarily on hold, college football fully came of age in the 1920s, when it became widely recognized as America's greatest sporting spectacle (as opposed to baseball, which was the national pastime). The first football stadiums at Harvard, Yale, and Princeton were modeled on the ancient Greek stadium and the Roman Colosseum, their architecture revealing much about football's cultural status. With a stadium-building boom in the 1920s, attendance more than doubled, exceeding 10 million by the end of the decade.

Newspaper coverage of the sport expanded at a similar rate. The daily newspaper had played a crucial role in the 1880s and '90s, introducing football to a popular audience with no connection to universities and their teams. Commercial radio appeared in 1920 and began regularly broadcasting football games a year later. By the end of the decade three networks were broadcasting a slate of games each Saturday, and local stations were covering all the home teams' games. By 1929 five newsreel companies were devoting roughly one-fifth to one-fourth of their footage to football in the fall. General-interest magazines such as *Collier's* and the *Saturday Evening Post* regularly published articles by or about famous coaches or players, along with short stories about the star who wins both the girl and the big game. Movie theaters each fall screened a handful of college football musicals and melodramas with kidnapped heroes who escaped just in the nick of time to score the winning touchdown.

RED GRANGE AND PROFESSIONALISM

The 1920s saw the emergence of Red Grange as football's first true celebrity. Grange received national acclaim for his brilliant performances in games against Michigan and Pennsylvania, but he also created the sport's greatest controversy since the 1906 rule changes when he left the University of Illinois (without graduating) to join the Chicago Bears of the professional NFL. "Professionalism" in any form—the paying of coaches, the recruiting and subsidizing of athletes, the commercializing of the supposedly amateur game—violated the sport's purported principles, yet it was also at the heart of the popular spectacle staged in the enormous stadiums before as many as 120,000 spectators. College football was regularly attacked in intellectual journals, but the routine celebration of the game in the daily and weekly coverage of the popular media drowned out any criticism. A report by the Carnegie Foundation in 1929 documenting professionalism at 84 of 112 institutions troubled many college administrators but was generally shrugged off by the public and the sportswriters who fed its passion for the game.

RED GRANGE

(b. June 13, 1903, Forksville, Pa., U.S.—d. Jan. 28, 1991, Lake Wales, Fla.)

An outstanding halfback whose spectacular long runs made him one of the most famous players of the 20th century, Red Grange was an important influence in popularizing professional football.

Harold Edward Grange was a star football player at Wheaton (Ill.) High School before entering the University of Illinois in 1922. There he played football during the 1923–25 seasons and was selected as an All-American halfback each season. He became a national idol in 1924 when he turned in one of the most sensational single-day performances by an athlete in sports history. Against a highly rated Michigan team, Grange ran for touchdowns of 95, 67, 56, and 44 yards in the first quarter of play. In the second half he scored a fifth touchdown and threw a touchdown pass in a 39–14 Illinois victory. Grange was nicknamed the "Galloping Ghost" for his blinding speed and elusive running style.

The following year Grange delivered another spectacular performance in the East, where some sportswriters questioned his ability as well as the quality of Midwestern football. He led Illinois to a 24–2 victory over Pennsylvania, scoring three touchdowns and gaining 363 yards. After his last college game in 1925, Grange dropped out of school and signed a professional contract with the Chicago Bears. Amid much controversy over his decision to leave school and become a professional athlete, Grange drew huge crowds to the Bears' final games that NFL season and on an extended barnstorming tour. He demonstrated the potential for the growth of pro football, a game that was not highly regarded at the time by many sports fans.

In 1926 Grange played for the New York Yankees in the American Football League, which he and his agent, Charles C. Pyle, founded. The league folded after one season, and the Yankees joined the NFL in 1927. Early that season Grange sustained a serious knee injury. He sat out the 1928 season, then returned to play for the Chicago Bears (1929–34). After his injury Grange was no longer the explosive runner he had been, but he remained a leading rusher in the NFL for a number of seasons and was also an excellent defensive back.

After his retirement from football, Grange became the first well-known athlete to become a successful radio and television broadcaster, with a career that spanned 25 years (1934–69). Grange was a charter member of both the College Football Hall of Fame (1951) and the Pro Football Hall of Fame (1963).

THE CREATION OF BOWL GAMES

In the 1920s and '30s colleges and universities throughout the Midwest, South, and West, in alliance with local civic and business elites, launched campaigns to gain national recognition and economic growth through their football teams. They organized regional conferences—the Big Ten and the Big 6 (now the Big 12) in the Midwest; the Southern, Southeastern, and Southwest conferences in the South; and the Pacific Coast Conference (now the Pacific-10) in the West—and scheduled "intersectional" games with regional prestige at stake. The Rose Bowl in Pasadena, California, on New Year's Day, first contested in 1902 between Stanford and Michigan, then annually beginning in 1916, determined an unofficial national champion and was also a highly profitable commercial enterprise.

The Pasadena Tournament of Roses is the oldest American postseason college football contest, held annually in Pasadena, Calif. The first such festival, originally called the Battle of Flowers, was held on Jan. 1, 1890. Under the auspices of the Valley Hunt Club, it consisted of a parade of local citizens decorating their carriages and buggies with flowers and driving over a prearranged route, followed by amateur athletic events. (While the first football game was held in Tournament Park in 1902, chariot races and other contests were thereafter substituted until football was introduced as the annual contest until 1916.) Beginning in 1897, the tournament was conducted by a newly established Pasadena Tournament of Roses Association.

Each Rose Bowl game is preceded by a Tournament of Roses Parade, or Rose Parade, which is one of the world's most elaborate and famous annual parades. The morning parade now consists of about 60 floats of intricate design, elaborately decorated with flowers and illustrating some aspect of the parade's theme of the year. Interspersed among the floats are marching bands and costumed horses and riders, and included in the 5.5-mile- (8.9-km-) long procession are a grand marshal and a Rose queen.

The Rose Bowl stadium opened in 1922, in time for the 1923 game. (Because of restrictions on crowds on the West Coast during World War II, the 1942 game was relocated to Durham, N.C.) Originally, the championship team of the Pacific Coast Intercollegiate Athletic Conference simply invited a winning team from anywhere in the eastern United States to be its opponent. Beginning in 1947, however, the Rose Bowl brought together teams from the Big Ten and Pacific-10 conferences and their forerunners. With the advent of the Bowl Championship Series system in 1998, the Rose Bowl has loosely maintained its tie-in with these two conferences, generally matching their champions unless one or both of them play in the national championship.

Soon after the advent of the Rose Bowl, promoters in other Sun Belt cities developed rival bowl games—the Orange Bowl in Miami (1933), the Sugar Bowl in New Orleans (1935), and the Cotton Bowl in Dallas (1937)—eventually to be joined by so many others that the NCAA in the 1950s began to regulate them.

KNUTE ROCKNE AND THE INFLUENCE OF COACHES

A distinguishing mark of American football is the renown and status granted to the most successful and innovative coaches. The first innovators were men such as Walter Camp (not literally a coach but an adviser), Amos Alonzo Stagg at the University of Chicago, George Woodruff at Pennsylvania, and Lorin Deland at Harvard, the coaches who developed the V trick, ends back, tackles back, guards back, flying wedge, and other mass formations that revolutionized, and nearly destroyed, the game in the 1890s. The most influential of the early coaches was Pop Warner, whose wingback formations (the single wing and the double wing), developed at Carlisle, Pittsburgh, and Stanford, became the dominant offensive systems through the 1930s.

Notre Dame teams of the 1920s and 1930s were immensely popular nationwide thanks, in part, to their charismatic coach, Knute Rockne (seated, in train). New York Daily News/Getty Images

POP WARNER

(b. April 5, 1871, Springville, N.Y., U.S.—d. Sept. 7, 1954, Palo Alto, Calif.)

Not only did Pop Warner devise the dominant offensive systems used over the first half of the 20th century, but in more than 44 years as a coach (1895–1938), he won 319 games, the most in the NCAA until the 1980s. He also is remembered for having given his name to one of the country's major football organizations for young boys, the Pop Warner Youth Football League, in 1934.

At Cornell University (N.Y.), Glenn Scobey Warner excelled in several sports while obtaining his law degree (1894). He then coached at the University of Georgia (1895–96) and Cornell (1897–98) before accepting a position at the Carlisle (Pa.) Indian Industrial School, where he coached from 1899 through 1903 and 1907 through 1914 (returning to Cornell for the three seasons between the two stints). After complaints from players about his profanity and abusive treatment led to Warner's dismissal from Carlisle, he coached at the University of Pittsburgh (1915–23), winning two unofficial national championships; at Stanford University (1924–32) in California, where his teams played in three Rose Bowls; and finally at Temple University (1933–38) in Philadelphia.

Warner's popular image is most closely tied to his association at Carlisle with Jim Thorpe, their relationship immortalized (and romanticized) in the 1951 film *Jim Thorpe—All-American*. But his chief contributions to football were the wingback formations he introduced at Carlisle and further developed at Pittsburgh and Stanford. In the single wing the ball was snapped to a tailback lined up behind the centre about five yards deep, with the fullback, quarterback, and wingback to one side, each a little wider than the last and closer to the line. Warner generally used an unbalanced line; that is, he placed four linemen to the side of the centre where the backs were lined up in order to further strengthen the running attack to that side. The less-popular double wing, developed at Stanford, was a more balanced formation, with the quarterback shifted into a wingback position on the side opposite from the other backs. Over the 1940s and '50s, Warner's single wing was gradually replaced by the split-T as the dominant offensive system.

The only rival to Pop Warner's wing formations in the 1920s and '30s was the Notre Dame box, Knute Rockne's refinement of the shift from the T to a box-shaped formation that was first developed by Stagg. A series of rule changes eventually rendered the box shift ineffective, but Rockne, football's first celebrity coach, was less an innovator than a master teacher and motivator. Under his guidance, Notre Dame developed the dominant football program in the country. It was the only team of the era with a nationwide following and the benchmark against which others were measured.

Rockne accomplished this under most unpromising circumstances. The 1920s were marked by anti-Catholic and anti-immigrant prejudice in much of the country, and Notre Dame's teams were decidedly Roman Catholic and ethnic. College football was transformed in the 1920s and '30s by the sons of Italian, Polish, Jewish, and other southern and eastern European immigrants, most conspicuously in the lineups of Catholic universities (Fordham, St. Mary's, and more than a dozen others in addition to Notre Dame) and the state universities in Pennsylvania and the upper Midwest. Known as the Ramblers or the Nomads (the "Fighting Irish" nickname was adopted in the late 1920s), the Notre Dame team developed a national schedule out of necessity rather than design. Refused games by nearby Big Ten rivals, Rockne scheduled contests with Army, Georgia Tech, Southern California, Southern Methodist, Nebraska— an entire intersectional schedule rather than a key game or two. The university's administrators soon recognized the advantages to be had, as Notre Dame became the representative school for Catholics and new immigrants throughout the country. In an era of university-building through big-time football, Notre Dame became the model that many others sought to emulate.

Initially the paying of coaches was controversial, as yet another mark of professionalism in the amateur sport, and there was always resistance to coaches' increasing control over the game. Rules to prevent sideline coaching—sending in plays from the sidelines—were first established in 1892 and not abandoned altogether until 1967. After free substitution was permitted during World War II because of the wartime manpower shortage, a postwar controversy over one-platoon or two-platoon football (11 men playing both ways, or separate squads for offense and defense) arose in part out of concern that coaches not gain more control over the game. The colleges returned to one-platoon football in 1953, but in 1965 open substitution and two platoons returned to stay, and coaches soon took over all of the play calling. Successful coaches were well compensated, often earning more than full professors by the 1920s (a time when such disparities were controversial) and eventually more than college presidents; this trend culminated in the million-dollar—and even multimillion-dollar—salaries of the 21st century.

CHAPTER 2
THE CHANGING
FACE OF FOOTBALL

As college football thrived in the early 20th century, professional football struggled for respectability. To the American sporting public at the time, football was inextricably linked to the university setting. Walter Camp developed the modern game on a college campus, professionalism purportedly undermined the sport's core principles, and certain college football games were already established annual traditions by the end of World War I. But the uphill battle proved quite winnable for the pro game, as it became—by a good measure—the dominant version of the sport by the end of the century.

BIRTH AND EARLY GROWTH OF PROFESSIONAL FOOTBALL

The group of teams that became the NFL was organized in 1920 as the American Professional Football Association (changing its name in 1922), with Jim Thorpe as its nominal president. Former (and sometimes current) college stars had played for money since 1892, initially for athletic clubs in western Pennsylvania, then for the openly professional teams that were formed in mostly small towns in Pennsylvania, Ohio, and Illinois. In its first season, in 1920, the APFA had 14 teams, including George Halas's Decatur (Ill.) Staleys, who in 1922 became the Chicago Bears, the NFL's dominant team for much of its formative period.

Joe Carr, an experienced promoter, succeeded Thorpe as president in 1921 and remained in that position until his death in 1939. Over the 1920s and early 1930s, league membership fluctuated between eight and 22 teams, the majority not in large cities but in towns such as Akron, Canton, Dayton, and Massillon, all in Ohio; Racine, Wisconsin; and Rockford, Illinois. With professionalism widely regarded as the greatest danger to college football, professional football was little more respectable than professional wrestling. Red Grange's turning professional in 1925 provided a temporary boost to the professional game, but interest in professional football could be sustained only in those communities with franchises.

The NFL took its modern shape in 1933 under Carr's guidance, when it was reorganized in two five-team divisions of big-city clubs (with Green Bay the lone exception) whose leaders would meet at the end of the season for the NFL title. In the 1930s professional football was predominantly a working-class spectator sport. The preseason College All-Star Game, created by *Chicago Tribune* sports columnist Arch Ward in 1934 to pit the reigning NFL champion against a team of just-graduated collegians, helped break down the barrier between college and professional football. Over the 1930s and '40s the professional sport's popularity grew in NFL cities, particularly those such as New York without a major state university with which to compete for the community's loyalty. Minor professional leagues such as the American Association, Dixie League, and Pacific Coast Professional Football League had relatively modest local followings.

The NFL was also successful enough to attract competitors. The American Football League was formed in 1926 by Grange and his agent, but it lasted just one year. A second (1936–37) and third (1940–41) AFL were also formed.

JIM THORPE

Jim Thorpe in his playing days with football's Canton (Ohio) Bulldogs. Hulton Archive/Getty Images

(b. May 28, 1888, near Prague, Indian Territory [now in Okla.], U.S.—d. March 28, 1953, Lomita, Calif.)

One of the most accomplished all-around athletes in history, Jim Thorpe was selected by American sportswriters and broadcasters in 1950 as the greatest American athlete and the greatest football player of the first half of the 20th century.

Predominantly of American Indian (Sauk and Fox) descent, James Francis Thorpe attended Haskell Indian School in Lawrence, Kansas, and Carlisle (Pa.) Indian Industrial School. While playing football for Carlisle under coach Pop Warner, he was chosen as halfback on Walter Camp's All-America teams in 1911 and 1912. He was a marvel of speed, power, kicking, and all-around ability. Also in 1912 Thorpe won the decathlon and the pentathlon by wide margins at the Olympic Games in Stockholm, but in 1913 an investigation by the Amateur Athletic Union showed that he had played semiprofessional baseball in 1909 and 1910, which should have disqualified him from Olympic competition. He was subsequently stripped of his gold medals.

From 1913 through 1919, Thorpe was an outfielder for the New York, Cincinnati (Ohio), and Boston baseball teams in the National League. He was more successful as one of the early stars of American professional football from 1919 through 1926. He spent two seasons (1922–23) with the Oorang Indians, whose owner attracted crowds by having Thorpe and his teammates dress up and perform "Indian" tricks before games and at halftime. In 1920–21 he served as the first president of the American Professional Football Association (later the NFL). He also excelled in such diverse sports as basketball, boxing, lacrosse, swimming, and hockey.

In his later years, even as he was celebrated in magazine and newspaper articles as one of the greatest athletes of all time, alcoholism and inability to adjust to employment outside sports reduced Thorpe to near poverty. The 1951 film biography of his life, titled *Jim Thorpe— All-American* and starring Burt Lancaster, transformed his story into uplifting melodrama, with the fallen hero rescued by his old coach Pop Warner.

In 1954, after his death, the communities of Mauch Chunk and East Mauch Chunk, Pennsylvania, merged to form the borough of Jim Thorpe. From 1955 the Jim Thorpe Trophy was awarded annually to the most valuable player in the NFL. In 1973 the Amateur Athletic Union restored his amateur status, but the International Olympic Committee did not recognize his amateur status until 1982. Thorpe was subsequently restored as a "cowinner" of the decathlon and pentathlon of the 1912 Olympic Games (along with the second-place finishers in those events). His Olympic gold medals were restored to his family in 1983.

Finally, the All-America Football Conference (1946–49) seriously challenged the existing league and contributed the Cleveland Browns, San Francisco 49ers, and a first version of the Baltimore Colts to an expanded NFL in 1950. Yet professional football could offer the public nothing comparable to the compelling rivalries, youthful enthusiasm, and colourful pageantry of college football. It was only in the 1950s with the arrival of television that professional football could reach beyond the franchise cities to become a national sport.

THE RACIAL TRANSFORMATION OF AMERICAN FOOTBALL

Through the end of World War II, very few African American athletes had an opportunity to play mainstream football at any level. A separate and decid-edly unequal black football world first emerged in the 1890s as part of the larger expansion of college foot-ball. The first documented game between all-black colleges was played in 1892 in North Carolina between Biddle University and Livingston College. The first black college conferences, the Colored Intercollegiate Athletic Association and the Southern Intercollegiate Athletic Conference, were formed in 1912, followed by the Southwestern Athletic Conference in 1920 and the Midwestern Athletic Association in 1926. Black college football was woefully underfunded, but it had its own All-Americans (stars such as "Jazz" Byrd, Ben Stevenson, "Tarzan" Kendall, and "Big Train" Moody), its great rivalries (Howard-Lincoln, Tuskegee-Atlanta, Morgan-Hampton, Wiley-Prairie View), its own pageantry, and even its own scandals. All of this took place outside the consciousness of the mainstream football public but was thoroughly covered by a thriving black press.

Mainstream football, however, was not altogether segregated. William Henry Lewis and William Tecumseh Sherman Jackson were black teammates for Amherst College in 1889, and Lewis made Walter Camp's All-America team in 1892 after he had moved to Harvard to play football while attending law school (he later became an assistant U.S. attorney general). A handful of black players were always part of big-time college foot-ball, and some—including Lewis, Fritz Pollard at Brown, Paul Robeson at Rutgers, and Duke Slater at Iowa—were among the early game's greatest stars. Yet, until 1939, when UCLA fielded a team that included Jackie Robinson, Kenny Washington, and two other black teammates, no college had more than one or two black players, and most continued to have none.

FRITZ POLLARD

(b. Jan. 27, 1894, Chicago, Ill., U.S.—d. May 11, 1986, Silver Spring, Md.)

Fritz Pollard was the first African American selected to a backfield position on Walter Camp's All-America team (1916) and the first African American head coach in the NFL, with the Akron Pros in 1921.

Only 5 feet 7 inches (1.7 metres) and 150 pounds (68 kg), Frederick Douglass Pollard won the grudging acceptance of his teammates at Brown University in Rhode Island in 1915, leading the team to a victory over Yale and an invitation to the Tournament of Roses game in Pasadena, California. Pollard had a subpar game in a 14–0 defeat to Washington State, but he became the first African American to play in the Rose Bowl game. In 1916 Pollard's outstanding play led Brown to a season of eight victories and one defeat, including wins over both Yale and Harvard.

After service in World War I, Pollard became head football coach at Lincoln University (Pa.) and began playing professional football for Akron in the informal Ohio League in 1919. The following year Pollard was the star player for the Akron Pros, who won the first NFL championship. Pollard continued to play and coach in the NFL until 1926. In 1923, while playing for the Hammond Pros, he became the first African American quarterback in the league. Pollard also facilitated integration in the NFL by recruiting other African American players such as Paul Robeson, Jay Mayo Williams, and John Shelbourne and by organizing the first interracial all-star game featuring NFL players in 1922.

After he was let go by Akron (which had changed its name to the Indians) in 1926, Pollard continued to promote integration in professional football as a coach of the barnstorming Chicago Black Hawks (1928–32) and the New York Brown Bombers (1935–37). In 1954 Pollard became the second African American selected to the College Football Hall of Fame. He was posthumously inducted into the Pro Football Hall of Fame in 2005.

The routine indignities facing the black pioneers on predominantly white teams and campuses became compounded when intersectional games were scheduled between segregated Southern schools and marginally integrated Northern ones. Typically, the Northern school agreed to "bench" its one or two black players so as not to offend Southern sensibilities. Such incidents occasionally aroused local protest from progressive student groups and were thoroughly covered in the black press, but they went largely unreported in the mainstream media. By the late 1930s the typical arrangement was to hold out the black players for games played in the segregated South but to allow them to play at home, an accommodation that continued into the 1950s.

The first integrated college football game in the South took place in 1947 between Virginia and Harvard, whose Chester Pierce was permitted to play. Many Northern schools solved the problem simply by not scheduling teams from the South, and bowl games likewise avoided racial incidents by matching up only Southern teams. The Cotton Bowl was integrated, without incident, in 1948, the Orange Bowl in 1955. The Sugar Bowl was integrated by the University of Pittsburgh's Bobby Grier in 1956, only after Georgia's segregationist governor, Marvin Griffin, backed down from threats to keep Georgia Tech from playing. The integration of Southern college teams progressed gradually over the postwar years. The Big 6 conference was integrated in 1947 and the Missouri Valley Conference in 1950; but the Atlantic Coast Conference did not begin integrating until 1963, the Southwest Conference until 1966, and the Southeastern Conference until 1967.

The NFL had been integrated at the beginning, with Fritz Pollard among the league's first stars and some 13 African American players hired between 1920 and 1933. Between 1934 and 1945, however, a "gentleman's agreement," apparently at the instigation of George Preston Marshall, owner of the Boston (later Washington)

Redskins, kept the NFL all-white. The reintegration of professional football began in 1946 — in the NFL, where the Rams risked losing their lease on the Los Angeles Coliseum if they did not sign Kenny Washington (the Rams signed Woody Strode as well, to give Washington a black roommate); and in the rival All-America Football Conference, where coach Paul Brown immediately signed Bill Willis and Marion Motley for his Cleveland Browns — and it was completed in 1962, when Marshall signed Bobby Mitchell to play for the Redskins. The first generation of black NFL stars came almost exclusively from the mainstream football world, but in the 1960s NFL scouts discovered the black colleges, Eddie Robinson's Grambling Tigers in particular. This golden era for black college football was short-lived, however, as integration ended the black colleges' monopoly on local African American athletic talent.

THE ERA OF TELEVISION

Together with the racial integration of the game at all levels, the coming of television in the 1950s marked a new era in the development of American football. The 1950s were a boom time for professional football but a bad time for the colleges, yet intercollegiate football, too, emerged from the decade not only intact but on the verge of unprecedented prosperity.

Immediately following World War II, college football experienced a surge in popularity, but attendance declined by the end of the decade and recovered very slowly over the 1950s. Many colleges dropped the game as too expensive, including one-time powers such as Fordham and St. Mary's. The informally organized Ivy League became a formal organization in 1954, choosing to play a "deemphasized" brand of football. The National Association of Intercollegiate Basketball, created in 1940 by small colleges concerned about the state of amateurism in that sport, became the National Association of Intercollegiate Athletics (NAIA) in 1952 and first sponsored a national championship in football in 1956.

The colleges and universities that clung to the big-time game faced a double crisis: the impact of television on gate receipts and the final throes of the ongoing controversy over professionalism. The NCAA named its first executive director, Walter Byers, in 1951 (he continued in that role until 1987) and took on regulatory and enforcement powers for the first time. Regarding television not as the tremendous source of revenue it eventually became but as the most serious threat to gate receipts, the NCAA in 1951 assumed control of broadcasting rights and established severe restrictions on the number of times any team could appear on TV. Under NCAA control, while attendance grew from 20 million in 1961 to 35.8 million in 1981, TV revenues increased from $3 million to $31 million, then doubled in 1982 when the NCAA signed its final contract with the networks.

Divvying up these huge revenues nearly tore the NCAA apart—small schools sought a portion for themselves, while the major football powers resented sharing the income that they generated. The big schools also chafed as NCAA decision making was dominated by the more numerous smaller schools. University and college divisions were created within the NCAA in 1968, with 223 schools in the former and 386 in the latter. Then, at a special meeting in 1973, institutions were assigned to Divisions I, II, or III, based essentially on the size and ambitions of the football program. Subsequent conventions fought over the allocation of TV revenues among the divisions, and in 1977 the major football conferences (excluding only the

Pacific-8 and the Big Ten), along with the major independents such as Notre Dame, formed the College Football
Association (CFA) to challenge the NCAA's power. Faced
with the threat of the CFA, the NCAA at its 1978 convention split Division I into Division I-A (the big-time
football schools) and I-AA.

Still unsatisfied by the division of TV revenues under
the new arrangement, the CFA attempted to negotiate its
own TV contract in 1981. When the NCAA threatened
sanctions, the Universities of Georgia and Oklahoma sued
the organization for violating the Sherman Antitrust Act;
the University of Texas sued separately. By 1984 the plain-
tiffs had prevailed all the way to the U.S. Supreme Court,
and the NCAA no longer controlled TV contracts. The
CFA itself was undermined in 1990 when Notre Dame
broke ranks to sign its own contract with NBC, after
which individual conferences began negotiating separate
arrangements with the networks.

As a consequence of these varied actions, by the 1990s
television revenues were going almost entirely to the big
football schools, and major conference realignments—
Penn State joining the Big Ten in 1990, the Southeastern
Conference expanding to 12 teams in 1992, the Big 8 becoming the Big 12 in 1996 by absorbing four Texas schools from
the disbanded Southwest Conference—resulted in large
part from consideration of TV markets.

SCHOLARSHIPS AND THE STUDENT ATHLETE

College football's other post–World War II crisis, regarding professionalism, reached a flash point in the late 1940s
and early 1950s over athletic scholarships. Subsidizing
athletes had been common since the 1920s but was not
officially sanctioned and was entirely unregulated, controlled more often by alumni than by athletic departments.

When the NCAA took on the issue after World War II, the Big Ten and the Pacific Coast Conference lobbied for need-based scholarships that awarded on-campus jobs. The Southeastern and Southwest conferences led the campaign for open athletic scholarships, declaring the job plan merely hypocritical (entailing phony jobs that required no work).

The job plan bloc prevailed at the NCAA convention in January 1948, passing what became known as the Sanity Code, but battles at subsequent meetings led to its being rescinded at the 1951 convention, and the now-familiar athletic grant-in-aid was finally adopted in 1957. Also in 1951, most of Army's football team was dismissed for cheating on exams; and it had been revealed earlier in the year that basketball players at several major universities had accepted money from gamblers to shave points. Out of this morass of scandal, the NCAA emerged stronger than ever, solidifying its standing as the regulatory, investigative, and punitive organization that ruled collegiate sports.

Once the issue of financial support was resolved and the sport fully integrated, the players' status as student-athletes received sharper scrutiny. The NCAA first tied eligibility for athletic scholarships to academic success in high school in 1965 with its "1.6 rule," then replaced it with a 2.0 grade-point-average standard in 1973. When the group passed Proposition 48 in 1983, followed by Proposition 16 in 1992, which together set minimal grade-point averages in a high school core curriculum and scores on the Scholastic Aptitude Test for scholarships and freshman eligibility, it addressed one continuing controversy while provoking another—its disproportionate impact on African Americans.

The problems and convulsions of the larger society inevitably spilled over into college football. The racial turmoil of the late 1960s led to bitter confrontations between black players and white coaches at several universities, and drug problems arose periodically, ranging from the abuse of amphetamines in the 1970s to the more dangerous abuse of anabolic steroids in the 1980s. The passage of Title IX forced athletic departments to divert financial resources into sports for women as well as men and made the football team, with its huge number of scholarships but also its unique capacity to generate income, a focal point for debates over gender equity. The commercialization set in motion by television led to institutional partnerships with soft drink and shoe companies, corporate sponsorship of bowl games, and million-dollar contracts for football coaches who were expected to contend for national championships. The competing demands of the sport, as an extracurricular activity for student-athletes and as mass entertainment, remained at the heart of American college football at the turn of the 21st century.

BOWL GAMES AND THE NATIONAL CHAMPIONSHIP

Even as bowl games proliferated in the 1930s, '40s, and '50s, controversies shadowed them for their commercialization of the amateur sport and prolonging of the season at the expense of academics. Resistance disappeared when the financial windfall from the televised contests became a major source of revenue for the top teams and conferences. A new controversy emerged in the 1970s, however, regarding the bowls' inability to produce an unambiguous national champion. A perennial call for a national championship playoff, resisted by defenders of the traditional bowl games, eventually prompted the creation in 1992 of the Bowl Coalition—involving four major bowl games (Cotton, Fiesta, Orange, and Sugar), five major

THE BCS

The BCS (short for Bowl Championship Series) is an arrangement of five American college postseason football games that annually determines the national champion. The games involved are the Rose Bowl, the Orange Bowl, the Sugar Bowl, the Fiesta Bowl, and the BCS National Championship Game.

The teams that participate in the BCS are drawn from the Football Bowl Subdivision (FBS, formerly known as Division I-A) of the National Collegiate Athletic Association and are determined by a ranking system that consists of three equally weighted components: the *USA Today* Coaches' Poll, the Harris Interactive College Football Poll, and an average of six computer rankings. (The computer rankings are created by specially designed programs that take into account a number of variables, which may include, but are not limited to, win-loss record, strength of a team's schedule, game locations, and margin of victory.) The two teams that top the rankings at the end of the regular season meet in the BCS National Championship Game, which rotates its location between the sites of the four bowls and takes place a few days after the bowl game that is traditionally held at that site.

The 10 BCS participants are selected by the individual bowl committees from a pool that consists of the automatically qualifying champions of the six "major conferences" (the Atlantic Coast, Big East, Big 12, Big Ten, Pacific-10, and Southeastern conferences) and four at-large teams. There is also a stipulation that awards automatic BCS berths—at the expense of major conference at-large selections—to members of the five other conferences in the FBS if they are among the top 12 teams in the final BCS rankings. Moreover, by special arrangement, if the University of Notre Dame, a traditional football power that has no conference affiliation, is among the top eight teams in the final BCS rankings, it too receives an automatic berth.

The BCS is the first true postseason football championship arrangement in the history of the NCAA's highest division. Since the 1970s the NCAA's lower divisions—the Football Championship Subdivision (formerly Division I-AA), Division II, and Division III—and the National Association of Intercollegiate Athletics (NAIA) have determined their national champions through single-elimination tournaments with fields ranging from 16 to 32 teams. Previously, the title of Division I-A "national champion" was bestowed on the team (or teams) that ended the season atop one of the polls taken of a fixed pool of coaches or sportswriters. Conventionally, the teams ranked first in the Associated Press (AP), United Press International (UPI), and coaches' polls were given the greatest claim to the title, but various other polls also named national champions throughout the years. As a result, many seasons ended with split national champions. Because of contractual obligations between bowl games and conferences, postseason matchups between the two consensus top-ranked teams occurred in only 8 of the 57 seasons between 1936 (the first year of the AP poll) and 1992.

conferences (excluding the Big Ten and Pac-10), and independent Notre Dame—with the goal of matching the two top-rated teams in a championship game that would rotate among the four bowls.

In 1995 the Bowl Coalition was replaced by the Bowl Alliance (involving six conferences, Notre Dame, and only three bowls), but the nonparticipation of the Rose Bowl, Big Ten, and Pac-10 continued to leave the scheme badly flawed. In 1998 the Rose Bowl and its two participating conferences joined the Bowl Championship Series (BCS), which included all the major teams and conferences, with a supposed national championship game now rotating among the Rose, Orange, Sugar, and Fiesta bowls.

While the BCS and its forerunners produced matchups of the two top-ranked teams in the coaches' poll in 10 of the first 16 years of the system, the arrangements were not without controversy. The matching of the University of Nebraska with Miami in the 2002 Rose Bowl, after Nebraska had failed to win its own conference championship, made it clear that the BCS had not yet resolved the issue and guaranteed that a debate over a playoff along the lines of the NCAA basketball tournament would continue.

In 2003, because of its relatively low computer rankings, the University of Southern California was not selected to play in the national championship game despite having ended the regular season atop both the AP and coaches' polls. This resulted in the only split championship in the BCS era and led to the replacement of the AP poll by the Harris poll in the BCS formula. Many observers have agitated for the FBS to adopt a playoff format similar to that of the lower college football divisions, but the bowl tradition (more than 30 games played from just before Christmas to just after New Year's Day, usually in warm locales, attracting hundreds of thousands of vacationing fans) and the financial windfall provided by bowls make such a change unlikely.

ASCENDANCE OF THE NFL

Connected to a national audience through television—and under no obligation to build character or maintain educational standards—professional football became the most spectacular success story in the world of American sport over the second half of the 20th century. To an even greater degree than for college football, television became the professional sport's lifeblood, with increasingly lucrative television contracts guaranteeing large profits for every club no matter how well it fared on the field. In the 1950s, while college authorities fretted over television, NFL commissioner Bert Bell embraced it immediately and won congressional approval to black out television coverage in the cities where home teams were playing. In a stroke, Bell's efforts assured maximum attendance for the league's 12 clubs with little impact on the size of the league's rapidly growing TV audience. The televised championship game between the Baltimore Colts and New

Baltimore Colts quarterback Johnny Unitas (No. 19) throwing a pass during the 1958 championship game against the New York Giants. Robert Riger/ Hulton Archive/Getty Images

York Giants in 1958, decided in sudden death overtime, is widely recognized as the turning point in professional football's embrace by a national audience.

When Bell died in 1959, he was succeeded by the general manager of the Los Angeles Rams, Pete Rozelle, who became the most powerful and most effective commissioner in American professional sports. In addition to creating NFL Properties, which became a multibillion-dollar enterprise, Rozelle negotiated a series of contracts with the TV networks that grew from $4.65 million for the 1962 season to nearly $500 million per year when he retired in 1989, guaranteeing more than $17 million per club before a single fan bought a ticket. Most crucially, Rozelle persuaded Congress to continue granting the NFL exemptions from the Sherman Antitrust Act, allowing franchises to operate not as individual businesses but as a single entity, each club sharing equally in league-generated revenues. (In 2010 the U.S. Supreme Court ruled unanimously that the Sherman Antitrust Act did indeed apply to the NFL; by that time, however, the league had already established itself as the most powerful and profitable professional sports organization in the country.) Under Rozelle, the value of franchises increased from about $1 million in 1960 to more than $100 million in 1989, and under the structure he put in place franchise values exceeded $500 million by the end of the 20th century.

The NFL faced competition from a new rival in 1960, when the American Football League (AFL), backed by Texas billionaire Lamar Hunt, fielded teams in eight cities, three of them in direct competition with NFL franchises. A television contract with NBC gave the AFL a financial security none of its predecessors had had, and the NFL and AFL agreed to a merger in 1966, completed in 1970 with 26 clubs in two conferences. The pass-oriented AFL brought more excitement to professional football, as well as the game's most glamorous player, the New York Jets' quarterback Joe Namath. Out of the merger also came the Super Bowl, which soon became the single most popular and lucrative of all sporting events in the United States. Super Bowl I (not yet with that name) was played between the Green Bay Packers and the Kansas City Chiefs after the 1966 season, with more than 40 percent of the country's television sets tuned in to the two networks that broadcast the game. That percentage never dropped lower than 36, and it nearly hit 50 in 1982, as the game was eventually watched by as many as 130 million Americans in addition to a worldwide audience. The Super Bowl became a major civic ritual, as famous for its surrounding hoopla and million-dollar commercials as for the football games.

SHOWMANSHIP ON THE FIELD

Constant innovation held fan interest and kept it steadily increasing. Polls beginning in the early 1970s repeatedly identified professional football as Americans' favourite sport. Over the 1970s and '80s the NFL withstood the challenge of new rival leagues—the World Football League (1974–75) and the United States Football League (1983–85)—and invested in the Arena Football League (an indoor version of the sport that was played on a shortened field during the NFL's off-season from 1987 to 2008 and again from 2010 in a new incarnation) and expanded into Europe in 1991 with the World League of American Football (later NFL Europe; disbanded in 2007).

The African American athletes who increasingly dominated football also brought a new style to the game. The beginnings of end zone dances in the 1970s escalated into highly choreographed routines, followed by other attention-grabbing gestures by defensive as well as offensive players. These displays eventually led to rules against "excessive celebration" (in the NCAA as well as the NFL) and countercharges by African American spokesmen that the banned actions and gestures were not failures of sportsmanship but African American self-expression. Fans were divided between enjoyment of the antics and criticism for the loss of old-fashioned values, but the new flamboyance played well on television, and it made football more than ever an arena in which Americans dealt with shifting attitudes about race.

FRANCHISE SHIFTS AND FREE AGENCY

The two events most responsible for shaping the NFL for the 21st century took place off the field: a series of legal decisions established free agency for players and gave owners greater freedom to move their franchises. The growth of television revenues inevitably led the players to demand a fair share of the profits. In 1970 a brief training-camp strike by the NFL Players Association (formed in 1956 but relatively inactive until the 1970s) caused no disruption of the football season but foreshadowed more serious labor-management disputes to come. In 1974 a 41-day strike during training camp affected only preseason games, as the Players Association capitulated. More serious and prolonged strikes in 1982 (when the players were locked out for 57 days and the season was reduced to nine games) and 1987 (when a strike lasted 24 days, leading owners to cancel one game and hire "replacement" players for three more) were equally unsuccessful from the players' perspective but far more damaging to the image of the league.

A full quarter of the league's veteran players crossed picket lines in 1974, and in 1982 and 1987 those who refused to strike or who criticized the union included some of the game's top players. What the players lost on the picket line, they won in court, however, as a series of lawsuits finally forced the owners in 1993 to agree to free agency, with a salary cap (a limit on each club's expenditures on salaries). With players now able to change teams, salaries increased dramatically—from an average of $490,000 in 1992 to $663,000 in 1993 and reaching $1,896,000 by 2009—yet the clubs' financial stability and the competitive balance among teams were preserved by the salary cap and the college draft, which the Players Association made no attempt to challenge.

The NFL's other defeat in court benefited individual owners. In 1980 Al Davis, the managing general partner of the Oakland Raiders, successfully sued the NFL for not allowing him to move the Raiders to Los Angeles, where

A member of the Los Angeles Raiders takes a break from picketing during the 1987 NFL players strike. Mike Powell/Getty Images

he expected to make considerably more money (after leaving in 1982, Davis returned the Raiders to Oakland in 1995). The freedom to move franchises without league approval gave owners a powerful position in negotiating with city governments that viewed an NFL franchise as an essential foundation of community pride and the local economy. Numerous franchise shifts in the 1980s and '90s provoked local outrage but did not damage the league. At the turn of the 21st century, professional football was without question the most popular and the most profitable of American sports.

THE HISTORY OF CANADIAN FOOTBALL

The gridiron football played in Canada closely resembles the U.S. game, but it developed independently, and, overshadowed by ice hockey, it never achieved equal national importance.

Canadian football's earliest history remains uncertain. It is generally agreed that rugby came to Canada with British soldiers early in the 19th century, and games were reported in the *Toronto Globe* as early as 1859. Students at the University of Toronto were playing football by the early 1860s, but it was clubs in Quebec and Ontario, rather than universities as in the United States, that led the way in developing the sport. Several of these clubs formed the Foot Ball Association of Canada in 1873, adopting Rugby Union rules in 1875. This initial association collapsed in 1877, to be followed by the first of the Canadian Rugby Football Unions in 1880; the final one, the Canadian Rugby Union (CRU), formed in 1891. Provincial unions were likewise formed in Ontario and Quebec in 1883, but football developed later in the West, with the Western Canadian Rugby Football Union not forming until 1911. The top senior clubs—the Big Four of Quebec and Ontario (Ottawa, Montreal, Hamilton, and Toronto), together with the five top Western clubs (Winnipeg, Saskatchewan, Calgary, Edmonton, and British Columbia)—eventually formed the major football organization in Canada, the professional Canadian Football League.

The Grey Cup, named for Governor-General Earl Grey, was first awarded in 1909, with college and club teams alike competing. Over time, the Grey Cup became Canada's professional championship, as well as a week-long festival and the premier single sporting event in the country.

The CRU became the umbrella organization for all the football unions, including the Canadian Intercollegiate Rugby Football Union, which was formed by eight universities in 1897 in reaction to the growing professionalism among the top senior clubs. In addition to the championship for senior clubs, the CRU sponsored an intermediate championship beginning in 1894 and a junior championship beginning in 1908.

No clear boundaries between intercollegiate and club football, or even amateur and professional, were drawn in Canada for several decades, nor were football's commercial possibilities realized for some time. Unlike U.S. football, early Canadian football was a game for the players rather than the spectators. The University of Toronto's victory over the Parkdale Canoe Club for the initial Grey Cup, for example, drew 3,807 fans and generated gross revenues of $2,616.40. This was at a time when top U.S. university teams were playing before 50,000 spectators and Yale was earning more than $1 million from football.

Developing a uniform set of rules in Canada was far more difficult than in the United States. The U.S. model was a powerful influence that was resisted by those who desired to preserve the Canadian-ness of Canadian football. Though clinging to certain rugby features, the Canadian game was gradually "Americanized" by U.S. coaches such as Frank "Shag" Shaughnessy at McGill University (1912–29) and by pressure from Western clubs, which were more open to U.S. influence and to professionalism. The legalization of the forward pass in 1931 led clubs, particularly in the West, to seek U.S. players skilled at the passing game who were offered local employment in the midst of the Great Depression rather than direct payments.

An openly professional league, along the lines of the NFL, was first discussed in the 1930s, but it did not become a reality until after World War II. In 1935 the first-ever Western victory for the Grey Cup, by a Winnipeg club with nine U.S. players on the roster, marked a major turning point. The eastern-dominated CRU responded by establishing a residency requirement for players and limiting "imports" to five. The limit was raised from five to seven in 1950, then to eight in 1952, nine in 1954, and eventually 16. The top clubs formed their own Canadian Football Council (CFC) in 1956, dropping the name *rugby* altogether. The CFC became the Canadian Football League (CFL) in 1958 and withdrew from the CRU, with the four privately owned eastern clubs becoming the Eastern Football Conference in 1959 and the five community-run Western clubs becoming the Western Football Conference in 1961.

With the creation of the CFL, Canadian football at last took its modern form, with clearly differentiated professional and amateur versions. The CRU changed its name to the Canadian Amateur Football Association (CAFA) in 1966, when it also turned over trusteeship of the Grey Cup to the CFL; since 1986 CAFA has been known as Football Canada. As senior club football outside the CFL declined, the intercollegiate game, at a level comparable to (non-scholarship) Division III in the United States, became the chief amateur version. Provincial and regional intercollegiate athletic unions joined in a reconstituted Canadian Interuniversity Athletic Union (CIAU) in 1961 and changed its name to Canadian Interuniversity Sport (CIS) in 2001. Since 1967, conference champions have competed for the Vanier Cup in an annual Canadian College Bowl.

The CFL experienced a period of growth and relative stability in the 1970s and early 1980s, reaching an attendance record of 2,856,031 in 1983. Average salaries likewise increased, from $16,072 for imports and $10,920 for nonimports in 1970 to $72,259 and $53,189 in 1985. With more than eight million viewers making the Grey Cup the most-watched sporting event in Canada, television revenue reached $15.6 million for 1981–83 and $33 million for 1984–86.

Then came precipitous decline and turmoil. Faced with competition from televised NFL games and a persistent perception that home-grown football was second-rate, the CFL saw TV revenues fall to $240,000 per club by 1991. Montreal lost its original franchise in 1982, then its replacement in 1987. Deficit-burdened franchises did not move but repeatedly changed hands. The purchase of the Toronto Argonauts in 1991 by millionaire Bruce McNall, actor John Candy, and hockey great Wayne Gretzky marked the most conspicuous effort to produce first-class football with highly paid U.S. stars, but the experiment failed, and McNall and Gretzky sold the club in 1994 after Candy died.

Constantly fearing NFL expansion into Montreal and Toronto, CFL leaders had been discussing since the early 1970s their own expansion into the United States, which became a reality with teams in Sacramento (Calif.) in 1993 and Las Vegas (Nev.), Shreveport (La.), and Baltimore (Md.) in 1994, but the experiment failed after just three seasons. In 1996 the CFL reverted to an eight-team all-Canadian league, then returned to its original nine for the 2002 season. That configuration lasted only until 2006, when the Ottawa franchise folded. Stadium renovations by a number of teams in the early years of the 21st century increased attendance numbers league-wide, and simultaneous improved television revenues helped the CFL again become a profitable enterprise by 2010, with an eye toward expansion.

CHAPTER 3
PLAYING THE GAME

To the uninitiated, football can seem quite confusing. The advanced features of the game—plays, formations, and strategies—have been likened to chess in their complexity. Likewise, the fundamentals, such as scoring, downs, and penalties, are themselves far from readily apparent on initial viewings.

THE BASICS

The field for American football is 120 yards (109.8 metres) long, including two 10-yard (9.1-metre) end zones, and 53.33 yards (48.8 metres) wide. A coin toss at the beginning of the game determines who will put the ball in play with a place kick from the 30-, 35-, or 40-yard line (at the intercollegiate, professional, and scholastic levels, respectively) and which goal each team will defend.

Following the kickoff, the centre of the team in possession of the ball puts it in play by passing it between

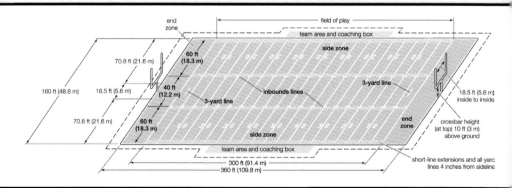

Football field according to NCAA specifications. Professional field varies slightly. Courtesy of the National Collegiate Athletic Association

PLAY IN CANADA

The play of Canadian football differs slightly from the U.S. version. The wider, longer field—150 yards (137.2 metres) by 65 yards (59.4 metres)—with 12 men on a side and only three tries for a first down (with the defense required to line up one yard behind the scrimmage line), encourages a more open style of play (laterals and passing rather than running). All offensive backs may be in motion when the ball is snapped (only one may in U.S. football). Blocking on punt returns is allowed only above the waist, and a kicked ball still in bounds must be played. One point (called a rouge) is scored if the team in possession kicks the ball over the defending team's goal line and the defending team fails to return the ball out of the end zone, which is 20 yards (18.3 metres) deep. The two-point conversion after a touchdown is attempted from the five-yard line.

his legs to the quarterback, who hands it off to another back, passes it to a receiver, or runs it himself. Opponents try to stop any advance toward their goal line by tackling the runner or by batting down or intercepting passes. The offensive team earns a "first down" by advancing the ball 10 yards in four downs or fewer and can retain the ball with repeated first downs until it scores or until the defense gains possession of the ball by recovering a fumble or intercepting a pass. Failing to make a first down, the offensive side must surrender the ball, usually by punting (kicking) it on fourth down.

SCORING

The offense scores by advancing the ball across the opponent's goal line (a six-point touchdown) or placekicking it over the crossbar and between the goal posts (a three-point field goal). After a touchdown, the ball is placed on the three-yard line (the two-yard line in the NFL), and

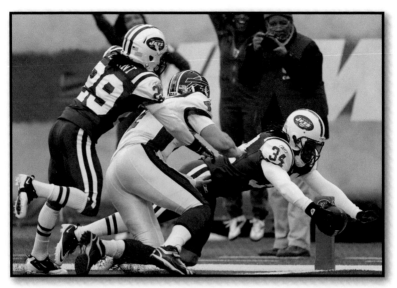

New York Jets player Marquice Cole (No. 34) reaches the ball across the goal line (known as breaking the plane) for a touchdown during a 2011 game against the Buffalo Bills. Al Bello/Getty Images

the scoring team is allowed to attempt a conversion: a placekick through the goal posts for one point or a run or completed pass across the goal line for two points.

The defense can score by returning a fumbled football or an interception across the other team's goal line for a touchdown, by tackling the ball carrier behind his own goal line (for a two-point safety), or by returning a failed conversion attempt across the opponent's goal line (two points).

TIME

Another kickoff, by the scoring team, follows each score, and the same pattern is repeated until playing time for the half expires (30 minutes for intercollegiate and professional football, 24 minutes for scholastic). After an intermission of 15 or 20 minutes, a second half follows, with the team that lost the initial coin toss choosing to kick or receive. The team that has scored the most points by the end of the game is the winner, and tie games are settled by additional play, determined by varying rules at the different levels.

Rules and Penalties

Detailed rules govern all aspects of the game: lining up and putting the ball in play, kicking and receiving, passing and defending against the pass, blocking and tackling. Penalties for infractions of the rules may be the loss of 5, 10, or 15 yards or half the distance to the goal line, the loss of down (for a foul committed by the offensive team), an automatic first down (for fouls against the defense), the awarding of the ball to the offended team at the spot of the foul, and disqualification. The most serious penalties are for various forms of excessive roughness.

The rules governing football in the NCAA, NFL, and NFHS have several minor variations. Time is stopped at the end of the first and third quarters, when the teams change goals. Each team is also allowed a number of optional timeouts, and time is automatically stopped for a variety of reasons during play and for commercials during televised contests. The result is that games last well beyond the actual playing time. In the NFL, games routinely exceed three hours.

Officiating

The game is supervised by seven officials in the NFL, four to seven in the colleges, and as few as three in high school. All officiating crews have a referee with general oversight and control of the game, who is assisted by umpires, linesmen, field judges, back judges, line judges, and side judges.

A referee, in the white cap, discusses a play with a head linesman. Referees are in charge of officiating football games, with support from umpires, linesmen, and judges. Greg Fiume/Getty Images

The referee is the sole authority for the score, and his decisions on rules and other matters pertaining to the game are final. The referee declares the ball ready for play and keeps track of the time between plays when it is not assigned to another official. He administers all penalties.

TACTICAL DEVELOPMENTS

The play on the field underwent continual innovation. Lacking the cachet of "college spirit," the NFL since the 1930s had always placed greater importance on entertainment. The NFL formed its own rules committee in 1933 and immediately moved the goal posts to the goal line (to make field goals easier), liberalized the rules on passing, and spotted the ball 10 yards from the sidelines when it went out of bounds. Until that time, the ball was placed at the sideline, and a play had to be wasted in order to move it to closer to the middle of the field.

Subsequent changes, in 1935 and 1972, eventually placed the ball even with the goal posts. (The colleges made similar changes but settled on a "hash mark" one-third of the field's width.) As the new rules opened up play, the Chicago Bears, under coaches George Halas and Ralph Jones, assisted by University of Chicago coach Clark Shaughnessy, reintroduced the old T formation, which eventually replaced the single wing as the dominant offensive formation. Quarterback Sammy Baugh and receiver Don Hutson elevated the passing game to new levels, while most college teams still played in a lower-scoring conservative style.

In the 1950s the Los Angeles Rams' head coach Sid Gillman exploited the passing game as never before, but in the late 1940s and '50s it was the Cleveland Browns' head coach Paul Brown who revolutionized professional football with organizational principles that were

GEORGE HALAS

(b. Feb. 2, 1895, Chicago, Ill., U.S.—d. Oct. 31, 1983, Chicago)

George Halas was the founder, owner, and first head coach of the NFL's Chicago Bears, which gave rise to his well-known nickname "Papa Bear." Halas revolutionized American football strategy in the late 1930s when he, along with assistant coach Clark Shaughnessy, revived the T formation and added to it the "man in motion" (a player moving prior to the start of a play).

After graduation from the University of Illinois in 1918, Halas served in the U.S. Navy and, in 1919, played major league baseball with the New York Yankees. In 1920 he organized the Decatur (Ill.) Staleys and helped to found the NFL. He moved the team to Chicago in 1921 and the following year renamed them the Bears. As a Bears player, he was an exceptional defensive end and set a league record by running 98 yards with a recovered fumble.

In 1930 he retired both as a player and as a coach, but he returned as a full-time coach in 1933. After his Bears, using the T formation, routed the Washington Redskins 73–0 in the 1940 championship game, the T quickly became the dominant offense in the NFL. From 1943 to 1945 he served in the navy once more. He returned to coach the Bears from 1946 through 1955 and from 1958 through 1967. Under his coaching, the Bears won seven league championships and four divisional titles. He again retired as coach in 1968, but he remained the chief executive officer of the Bears until his death.

Halas played an important role in the growth and success of the NFL. His signing of collegiate star Red Grange helped attract media attention to the struggling league. He also helped introduce such innovations to the game as public announcement systems and radio broadcasts. He was a charter member of the Pro Football Hall of Fame.

eventually adopted throughout the football world. Brown made the watching of game films a part of the entire team's preparation, placed assistant coaches in the press box, even experimented with implanting a radio transmitter in the quarterback's helmet—a tactic quickly banned by the commissioner, not to be legalized for another four decades. Brown invented "pocket protection" for his quarterback, with the linemen not aggressively blocking, as on running plays, but dropping back into a pocket to shield the quarterback. Vince Lombardi extended this principle to running plays at Green Bay in the 1960s, having his linemen block areas rather than specific men and having the running back read which way his lineman blocked his man at the point of attack. The basic principle of brushing defensemen aside rather than overpowering them gave new flexibility to the running game.

College football gradually adjusted to the more pass-oriented professional style. After World War II, college and professional coaches borrowed from each other, always looking for ways to exploit an offensive or defensive advantage. The Southwest Conference had been known for its wide-open passing attacks in the 1930s, but college football remained fundamentally a power running game into the 1980s. College coaches' most distinctive innovations in the 1970s and '80s came in offenses that featured running quarterbacks—the triple-option schemes such as the wishbone and veer (with the quarterback handing the ball off to a fullback, pitching it to a tailback, or keeping it himself), offenses that were unattractive to the pros because they put quarterbacks at physical risk.

The original defenses had simply mirrored the positions of the offense. In the 1930s a 6-2-2-1 alignment became dominant (6 linemen, 2 linebackers, 2 cornerbacks, and 1 safety). In the NFL, to stop the increased passing that came with the T formation in the 1940s, the Philadelphia Eagles' Greasy Neale developed the 5-3-2-1 defense, which was in turn replaced in the mid-1950s by the 4-3 (actually 4-3-2-2) perfected by Tom Landry as an assistant coach with the New York Giants. In this alignment the defensive tackles kept blockers off the middle linebacker, who became the dominant defensive player. The 4-3 defense made stars of such middle linebackers as Sam Huff, Joe Schmidt, Ray Nitschke, Dick Butkus, and Willie Lanier.

The 4-3, in turn, yielded to the 3-4 in the mid-1970s, moving the emphasis to outside linebackers rather than the middle linebacker. The New York Giants' Lawrence Taylor became the prototype outside linebacker in the 1980s, with tremendous speed to cover receivers and tremendous power to rush the quarterback. By the early 21st century both defensive alignments were in practice, with roughly equal use throughout the league.

Pass defenses had always been either man-to-man or zone (each back covering an area). In the 1970s, when zone defenses virtually eliminated long passes, strong running games—featuring backs such as Buffalo's O.J. Simpson, Miami's Larry Csonka and Jim Kiick, and Pittsburgh's Franco Harris and Rocky Bleir—dominated the NFL. Landmark rule changes in 1977—banning defensive contact with wide receivers more than five yards downfield and allowing offensive linemen to block with their open hands—returned the advantage to the passing offenses. Small, quick offensive linemen gradually disappeared, replaced by 300-pound (140-kg) hulks who could hold off charging pass rushers with their extended arms and hands. There were eight 300-pounders in the NFL in 1986 and 179 in 1996. In 2010, the vast majority of linemen in the league weighed more than 300 pounds.

Led by the so-called "West Coast offense" developed by Bill Walsh for the San Francisco 49ers, the passing game flourished as never before (in 1980 there were more passing than running plays for the first time since 1969). Other coaches developed run-and-shoot offenses, no-huddle offenses, and one-back offenses (with four wide receivers and no tight ends). Defensive coaches responded with "combo" pass defenses (combinations of zone and man-to-man), and the cornerback who could dominate a wide receiver by himself emerged as a new star. Deion Sanders became the prototype for this position. Running attacks increasingly featured a single back, making stars of such players as Tony Dorsett, Eric Dickerson, Walter Payton, Barry Sanders, Emmitt Smith, and LaDainian Tomlinson.

More so at the professional than the college level, football became increasingly specialized. To the kicking specialists who emerged in the 1960s were later added extra blockers for goal-line offenses, extra defensive backs for expected passing plays, and a variety of offensive and defensive specialists for the multiple alignments that all teams employed into the 21st century.

CHAPTER 4
THE NATIONAL FOOTBALL LEAGUE (NFL)

The National Football League is the major American professional football organization, founded in 1920 in Canton, Ohio, as the American Professional Football Association. Its first president was Jim Thorpe, an outstanding American athlete who was also a player in the league. The present name was adopted in 1922.

The league began play in 1920 and comprised five teams from Ohio (Akron Pros, Canton Bulldogs, Cleveland Tigers, Columbus Panhandlers, and Dayton Triangles), four teams from Illinois (Chicago Tigers, Decatur Staleys, Racine Cardinals [the Cardinals were based in Chicago but took the name of a local street], and Rock Island Independents), two from Indiana (Hammond Pros and Muncie Flyers), two from New York (Buffalo All-Americans and Rochester Jeffersons), and the Detroit Heralds from Michigan. Of these original franchises, only two remain. The Cardinals left Chicago for St. Louis after the 1959 season and relocated to Arizona in 1988. The Decatur Staleys moved to Chicago in 1921 and a year later changed their name to the Bears.

The NFL survived many years of instability and competition from rival organizations to became the strongest American professional football league. The most serious challenge to its leading role came from the American Football League (AFL) in the 1960s. The NFL and AFL completed a merger in 1970, creating a 26-team circuit under the name of the older NFL.

Since then the league has expanded four times, adding six new franchises. The league's 32 teams are aligned as follows:

National Football Conference (NFC)

- Eastern Division: Dallas Cowboys, New York Giants, Philadelphia Eagles, Washington Redskins
- Northern Division: Chicago Bears, Detroit Lions, Green Bay Packers, Minnesota Vikings
- Southern Division: Atlanta Falcons, Carolina Panthers, New Orleans Saints, Tampa Bay Buccaneers
- Western Division: Arizona Cardinals, St. Louis Rams, San Francisco 49ers, Seattle Seahawks

American Football Conference (AFC)

- Eastern Division: Buffalo Bills, Miami Dolphins, New England Patriots, New York Jets
- Northern Division: Baltimore Ravens, Cincinnati Bengals, Cleveland Browns, Pittsburgh Steelers
- Southern Division: Houston Texans, Indianapolis Colts, Jacksonville Jaguars, Tennessee Titans
- Western Division: Denver Broncos, Kansas City Chiefs, Oakland Raiders, San Diego Chargers

The league season culminates with an annual 12-team play-off tournament leading to the Super Bowl championship game. The NFL has headquarters in New York City and, since 1963, has maintained the Pro Football Hall of Fame in Canton, Ohio.

THE NATIONAL FOOTBALL CONFERENCE (NFC)

NFC EAST

DALLAS COWBOYS

Based in Dallas, the Cowboys are one of the NFL's most successful and popular franchises, having won five Super Bowls and eight conference championships.

The Cowboys joined the NFL as an expansion team in 1960 under head coach Tom Landry. After posting a losing record in each of their first five seasons, the Cowboys quickly became one of the NFL's better teams, qualifying for the play-offs in 17 of the 18 seasons between 1966 and 1983. The Cowboys joined the Detroit Lions in hosting an annual home game on Thanksgiving Day in 1966, a move that greatly increased the team's national exposure. In 1967 Dallas reached the NFL championship game but lost to the Green Bay Packers in a contest that featured the lowest recorded on-field temperature in NFL history (−13 °F [−25 °C]) and became known as the "Ice Bowl."

Future Hall of Fame quarterback Roger Staubach arrived in 1969 and went on to establish the Cowboys as a perennial title contender. With Staubach the Cowboys won five NFC championships and two Super Bowls (1972, 1978), and the popular franchise, which also boasted scantily clad cheerleaders who were both sex symbols and the targets of feminist scorn, became known by the nickname "America's team." Other notable players of the Landry era included defensive tackles Bob Lilly and Randy White, wide receiver and former Olympic sprint

Members of the Dallas Cowboys dig in to a sideline Thanksgiving feast in 2009. The Cowboys have become a Thanksgiving Day staple, playing on the holiday since 1966. Greg Nelson/Sports Illustrated/Getty Images

champion Bob Hayes, cornerback Mel Renfro, and running back Tony Dorsett.

Businessman Jerry Jones purchased the franchise in 1989 and fired Landry soon thereafter, earning the ire of the many loyal Cowboys fans who had grown attached to the coach in his 28 years with the team. The situation was ameliorated by the fact that the Cowboys had a string of excellent drafts at this time, acquiring future Hall of Famers Michael Irvin, Troy Aikman, and Emmitt Smith in successive drafts from 1988 to 1990. The team went on to dominate the NFL for the better part of the decade. The Cowboys of the 1990s won Super Bowls in 1993, 1994, and 1996.

The early part of the next decade saw the franchise decline as its stars retired or left for other teams. Though the Cowboys occasionally qualified for the postseason, they did not win a play-off game from 1996 until 2010, when quarterback Tony Romo—after guiding the Cowboys to a division

BOB LILLY

(b. July 26, 1939, Olney, Texas, U.S.)

Bob Lilly is considered one of the greatest defensive linemen in NFL history. As the anchor of the Dallas Cowboys' "Doomsday Defense," he helped the team win its first Super Bowl title (1972).

Robert Lewis Lilly was raised in rural Texas and moved with his family to Oregon shortly before his senior year of high school. He was named all-state in both football and basketball in his one year in the Pacific Northwest, and he earned an athletic scholarship to Texas Christian University (TCU). He was a consensus All-American in his senior season at TCU, and he became the first college draft choice in Cowboys history when the team selected him with the 13th overall pick of the 1961 draft.

Originally a defensive end, Lilly moved to defensive tackle during his third season, and he flourished as an interior lineman. He was named All-Pro in each season from 1964 to 1969 as the Cowboys—a winless expansion team in the year before Lilly's arrival—developed into one of the most formidable teams in the NFL. Lilly and the Cowboys played in six league or conference (after the NFL merged with the AFL in 1970) championship games in the eight-year period from 1966 through 1973. He helped the Cowboys reach their first Super Bowl (a loss to the Baltimore Colts) in 1971 and a second berth in the game the following year, when Lilly and the Doomsday Defense held the Miami Dolphins to just a field goal in Dallas's 24–3 win. Lilly retired in 1975.

The durable Lilly missed just one game over the course of his 14-year NFL career, a remarkable achievement for someone who played two of football's most grueling positions. After his retirement from football, he embarked on a successful career as a photographer. Lilly was inducted into the Pro Football Hall of Fame in 1980.

title during the 2009 regular season—led the team to an opening-round play-off victory over the Philadelphia Eagles.

NEW YORK GIANTS

Based in East Rutherford, N.J., the Giants have won four NFL championships (1927, 1934, 1938, 1956) and three Super Bowls (1987, 1991, 2008). The Giants are noted for their early successes and their dominant play in the 1980s and '90s under head coach Bill Parcells.

The Giants were established in 1925 in New York and played their first three decades at the Polo Grounds in upper Manhattan. The franchise was purchased for $500 by Tim Mara, whose family retained an ownership interest in the team into the 21st century. In 1930 Mara split ownership between his two sons, Jack and Wellington.

Although the Giants lost their first contest 14–0 to the Frankford Yellow Jackets, they quickly distinguished themselves as one of the great teams of early professional football, winning NFL championships in 1927, 1934, and 1938. The 1934 championship was won 30–13 over the Washington Redskins in the famous "Sneakers Game," wherein the Giants trailed at halftime but switched to basketball shoes to gain better traction on the icy field. During the next decade the Giants continued to enjoy success, advancing to (though losing) four NFL championship games (1939, 1941, 1944, 1946). In the late 1940s the team endured hardship on the field, posting consecutive losing seasons in 1947, 1948, and 1949 before enjoying success again in the 1950s.

In 1956 the Giants moved from the Polo Grounds to Yankee Stadium and, behind the legs of legendary running back Frank Gifford and the grit of linebacker Sam Huff, captured their fourth (and last) NFL championship. During this period the team included defensive back Emlen Tunnell, who played 11 seasons (1948–58) with the team and became the first African American player to be enshrined in the Pro Football Hall of Fame. The 1950s team was also notable for its coaching staff, with Vince Lombardi in charge of the offense and Tom Landry the defense. Both coaches went on to be legends of the Green Bay Packers and Dallas Cowboys, respectively.

The 1958 NFL championship pitted the Giants against the Baltimore Colts in what is viewed by many as one of football's greatest games. With a national television audience watching, the Colts beat the Giants 23–17 in a dramatic contest that ended in sudden-death overtime. The game marked the beginning of the NFL's tremendous popularity in the United States.

The Giants, led by quarterback Y.A. Tittle, advanced to the NFL championship game in 1961, 1962, and 1963 but then struggled for many seasons, posting only two winning records between 1964 and 1980 (1970, 1972). In that period the team also moved from New York to New Jersey, beginning play at Giants Stadium in the Meadowlands in 1976. (The team also played seasons in the Yale Bowl in Connecticut and Shea Stadium in Queens, N.Y.) During this stretch the Giants suffered one of their most stinging defeats in what was called the "Miracle at the Meadowlands" or "The Fumble." On Nov. 19, 1978, against the Philadelphia Eagles, the Giants led 17–12 and needed only to run out the clock to secure victory, but an errant handoff from quarterback Joe Pisarcik to fullback Larry Csonka allowed the Eagles' Herman Edwards to recover a fumble and run 26 yards into the end zone to win the game.

Bill Parcells became the Giants' head coach starting in the 1983 season. Parcells assembled teams that included linebackers Lawrence Taylor and Harry Carson, quarterback Phil Simms, and tight end Mark Bavaro. The Giants won Super Bowls following the 1986 and 1990 seasons, maintaining success through the majority of Parcells's tenure. After capturing the second Super Bowl, Parcells left the team. Afterward the Giants had a mixed record, with four winning seasons between 1991 and 2000. In 2000 they advanced to the Super Bowl, losing 34–7 to the Baltimore Ravens.

In 2004 Tom Coughlin joined the franchise as its head coach. Though he encountered occasional criticism for his no-nonsense coaching style, the Giants performed well under Coughlin's leadership. In 2008's Super Bowl XLII, led by quarterback Eli Manning and defensive lineman Michael Strahan, the Giants managed one of the greatest upsets in NFL history, defeating the previously undefeated and heavily favoured New England Patriots.

PHILADELPHIA EAGLES

Based in Philadelphia, the Eagles have won three NFL championships (1948, 1949, 1960) and have appeared in two Super Bowls (1981, 2005).

The Eagles were founded in 1933 when the remains of the defunct Frankford Yellow Jackets franchise was sold to a syndicate of Philadelphia-based businessmen. The team was not an early success, as it posted either one or two victories in seven of its first 10 seasons, but the hiring of head coach Earle "Greasy" Neale in 1941 marked the beginning of a turnaround in Philadelphia. Neale guided teams featuring star running back Steve Van Buren to an NFL championship game appearance in 1947 and NFL titles in 1948 and 1949. The Eagles slowly regressed in the wake of their consecutive championships, and by the mid-1950s they routinely finished in the bottom half of the league. In 1960 the Eagles, led by quarterback Norm Van Brocklin and diminutive flanker Tommy McDonald on offense and linebacker Chuck Bednarik on defense, rebounded to win the franchise's third NFL championship, a 17–13 victory over the Green Bay Packers.

The Eagles' renaissance proved to be short-lived, as the team entered into an 18-year play-off drought immediately after their championship season. Head coach Dick Vermeil was hired in 1976, and his emotional coaching style energized the Eagles (as well as their fans), resulting in four straight play-off berths from 1978 to 1981, with teams that featured the passing duo of quarterback Ron Jaworski and the towering (6 feet 8 inches [2.03 metres] tall) wide receiver Harold Carmichael. This span was high-lighted by Philadelphia's first Super Bowl berth in 1981, though they lost to the Oakland Raiders, 27–10.

Before the 1985 season, the Eagles made two sig-nificant additions: Randall Cunningham, a fleet-footed quarterback who would set the career record for rushing yards from his position, and Reggie White, a dominant defensive end who would retire as the NFL's all-time sack leader. However, their stellar individual play never trans-lated to team postseason success, as the Eagles won only one of the five play-off games in which the pair played between 1988 and 1992.

In 1999 the team hired head coach Andy Reid, who with his first draft choice selected quarterback Donovan McNabb. Reid and McNabb guided the Eagles to eight play-off berths in 10 years from their second season in Philadelphia, which included five trips to the NFC cham-pionship game and a Super Bowl appearance in 2005, but no titles. The pair had a tumultuous relationship on and off the field, and in 2010 McNabb was traded away.

WASHINGTON REDSKINS

Based in Washington, D.C., the Redskins have won two NFL championships (1937, 1942) and three Super Bowls (1983, 1988, 1992).

Founded in 1932 as the Boston Braves, the team changed its name the following year and played three seasons as the Boston Redskins before relocating to Washington in 1937. The Redskins acquired one of their most famous players the same year, when they drafted groundbreaking quarterback Sammy Baugh with the sixth selection of the NFL draft. Baugh led the Redskins to a championship in his rookie season and set numerous NFL passing records over the course of his 16-year career. His second NFL championship with the Redskins came

SAMMY BAUGH

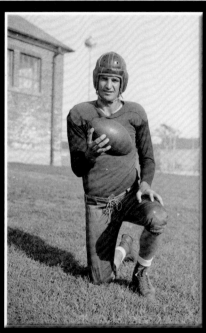

Sammy Baugh, 1937. Harris & Ewing Collection/Library of Congress, Washington, D.C. (Digital File Number: LC-DIG-hec-29054)

(b. March 17, 1914, Temple, Texas, U.S.—d. Dec. 17, 2008, Rotan, Texas)

Sammy Baugh was the first outstanding quarterback in the history of American professional football. He played a major role in the emergence of the forward pass as a primary offensive tactic in the 1930s and '40s. "Slingin' Sammy" led the NFL in passing in 6 of his 16 seasons (1937–52) with the Washington Redskins. He also excelled as a punter and as a defensive back. In 1943 he led the NFL in passing, punting, and interceptions (as a defensive back).

At Texas Christian University, in Fort Worth, Samuel Adrian Baugh became the top passer in the Southwest Conference, a league noted for its wide-open offenses at a time when most football teams used the forward pass only sparingly. He led his team to a victory in the 1936 Sugar Bowl, helping to bring national attention to the conference and to football in the Southwest for the first time. Baugh was named a consensus All-American in his senior season.

After graduation in 1937, Baugh joined both the Redskins and the St. Louis Cardinals baseball organization, for which he played shortstop in the minor leagues for a few years. Baugh led the NFL in completions and passing yards per game in his first season and helped Washington to an 8–3 record and a spot in the championship game, where he threw three touchdown passes in a 28–21 upset of the Chicago Bears. Behind Baugh, the Redskins played in four more championship games, capturing a second title in 1942. He led the NFL in passing yards per game again in 1938, 1940, 1945, 1947, and 1948 and in average yards per punt in 1940–43. As a defensive back, he led the NFL in 1943 by intercepting 11 passes, which remains one of the highest single-season totals in league history. He had career aggregates of 1,693 pass completions in 2,995 attempts (56.5 percent) for 21,886 yards and 187 touchdowns, all of which were NFL records at the time of his retirement.

Baugh was head coach of two AFL teams, the New York Titans in 1960–61 and the Houston Oilers in 1964. He was a member of the Pro Football Hall of Fame's inaugural class in 1963.

in 1942, as Washington defeated the Chicago Bears for the title two years after being humiliated in the championship game by the Bears 73–0.

One of the wealthiest NFL franchises, the Redskins, under the guidance of their owner, Hall of Famer George Preston Marshall, used their significant means to pioneer the use of sports broadcast media. In 1944 they assembled a radio network to broadcast games throughout the southern United States, and by 1950 the entire Redskins season was televised. The Redskins also have some of the most passionate fans in professional football; since 1967 the team has sold out every season, the longest string of sold-out games in the NFL.

The rise of the Redskins as a media power somewhat surprisingly coincided with the least successful period in team history. The Redskins posted just four winning records between 1946 and 1970, failing to advance to the play-offs in each season. Two notable players of this era were quarterback Sonny Jurgensen and wide receiver Bobby Mitchell, who starred for the Redskins in the 1960s and were inducted together into the Hall of Fame in 1983. In 1971 Washington hired head coach George Allen, who promptly led the team to a postseason appearance in his first year at the helm. The team's greatest success under Allen came in 1972. With a squad featuring wide receiver Charley Taylor on offense and linebacker Chris Hanburger on defense, the Redskins won their first NFC championship, only to lose the Super Bowl to the undefeated Miami Dolphins the following January.

In 1981 the team hired head coach Joe Gibbs, winner of more games than any other coach in Redskins history. Gibbs's record includes eight play-off appearances and four NFC championships along with three Super Bowl victories (1983, 1988, 1992). A testament to Gibbs's coaching ability—and to the overall quality of his teams—is the fact that each of the Redskins Super Bowl–winning teams was led by a different quarterback: Joe Theismann, Doug Williams, and Mark Rypien. Running back John Riggins, wide receiver Art Monk, and cornerback Darrell Green— all future Hall of Famers—starred for the Redskins during their Super Bowl–winning run, which was also famous for featuring rugged offensive lines known by the nickname "The Hogs." Gibbs retired in 1993, and the team promptly posted three consecutive losing seasons.

In 1999 the Redskins, owned outright since 1985 by the flamboyant Jack Kent Cooke, were purchased by billionaire Daniel Snyder, whose ownership has been marked by splashy free agent acquisitions, as well as a four-year return to the sidelines by Gibbs beginning in 2004, but few winning seasons.

NFC Central

Chicago Bears

Based in Chicago, the Bears are one of football's most successful franchises, having won eight NFL championships and one Super Bowl. The Bears have more former players in the Pro Football Hall of Fame (26) than any other team.

The franchise that became the Bears was founded by businessman A.E. Staley in 1920 and was first known as the Decatur (Ill.) Staleys. George Halas became player-coach of the new team, which he relocated to Chicago in 1921 after Staley handed the young franchise over to him. (Halas, affectionately known as "Papa Bear," prowled the sidelines as head coach until 1968.) The team won the American Professional Football Association (APFA) championship in its first season in Chicago, and it was renamed the Bears in 1922, the same year the APFA became the NFL.

The early Chicago teams established a rivalry with the Green Bay Packers, which became one of the sport's most storied feuds. Led by a dominant rushing attack that featured future Hall of Fame backs Red Grange and Bronko Nagurski, the Bears captured NFL championships in 1932 and 1933, the former of which was won in the first play-off game in league history, a 9–0 victory over the Portsmouth (Ohio) Spartans. In the 1940s the Bears won four more championships (1940, 1941, 1943, 1946), largely because of the efforts of quarterback Sid Luckman, a future member of the Hall of Fame. The innovative T-formation offense that Luckman ran, which utilized two running backs and set men in motion before the play, was an immediate sensation and became the dominant offense in the NFL.

The Bears won another title in 1963 and drafted two all-time greats in 1965: linebacker Dick Butkus and running back Gale Sayers. While Butkus and Sayers went on to dominate the game on an individual level, the Bears did not advance to the play-offs during either of their careers. The dry spell ended when the Bears drafted running back Walter Payton in 1975, starting a decade of dominance. Payton went on to break Jim Brown's record for all-time

BRONKO NAGURSKI

(b. Nov. 3, 1908, Rainy River, Ont., Can.—d. Jan. 7, 1990, International Falls, Minn., U.S.)

At 6 feet 2 inches (1.88 metres) and 226 pounds (102.5 kg), Bronko Nagurski was an unusually big player for his era and its quintessential bruising fullback.

Bronislau Nagurski's family relocated from Canada to the United States when he was a young boy, and he acquired his unique nickname as a result of his schoolmates' futile attempts to pronounce his name. He played tackle and end on defense and fullback on offense at the University of Minnesota (1927–29) and was named All-American at tackle in 1929. Nagurski became a legendary figure during his collegiate years. An oft-repeated tale that circulated through the popular press described Nagurski's discovery by his college coach. Lost on a recruiting trip, the coach asked a strapping farmer for directions to the nearest town, and the farmer, young Nagurski, pointed the way— with his plow.

In 1930 Nagurski joined the Chicago Bears. Playing fullback, he used his skill as a rusher, passer, and blocker to help the Bears win NFL championships in 1932 and 1933. He retired in 1937 because of a salary dispute and the unwillingness of the Bears management to allow him to wrestle professionally, which paid better. He continued to wrestle until 1942, but in 1943 he returned to the Bears, who were in need of players because of the manpower demands of World War II (Nagurski himself was passed over for service due to his damaged knees and ankles). Playing mostly tackle, Nagurski helped the Bears win the NFL championship that season. He left the sport at the end of the season and returned to wrestling, from which he retired in 1960. Nagurski was enshrined in the Pro Football Hall of Fame in 1963, as a member of that institution's inaugural class.

rushing yards (which was in turn broken by Emmitt Smith in 2002) and was elected into the Pro Football Hall of Fame in 1993. Behind Payton the Bears won four division titles and their only Super Bowl (1985).

Led by head coach Mike Ditka, a larger-than-life personality who had starred as a tight end for the Bears of the

Members of the Chicago Bears filming their 1985 music video, "The Super Bowl Shuffle." The video made the Bears national celebrities even before the team won the title the following January. Paul Natkin/NFL/Getty Images

1960s, and inconoclastic quarterback Jim McMahon (the "punky QB"), the 1985 Bears team was especially noteworthy for its overpowering defense that—after serving as the catalyst for a 15–1 regular-season record—allowed only 10 total points in the team's three postseason games. The team became a national sensation with the release of "The Super Bowl Shuffle," a rap song (and accompanying music video) that featured members of the team boasting of going to the Super Bowl, which was confidently released before the end of the regular season. The Bears experienced limited success after the early 1990s, but they did advance to the Super Bowl in 2006, where they lost to the Indianapolis Colts. Following the 2010 regular season, the Bears made it all the way to the NFC championship game, only to be felled by the Green Bay Packers, 21–14.

DETROIT LIONS

Based in Detroit, the Lions have won four NFL championships (1935, 1952, 1953, 1957).

The franchise, founded in 1930, was originally based in Portsmouth, Ohio. Known as the Spartans, the team was one of two (with the Green Bay Packers) small-town members of the early NFL. The Spartans were moderately successful and played in the first play-off game in league history—a 9–0 loss to the Chicago Bears at the end of the 1932 season. In 1934 the franchise was sold and relocated to Detroit, where it took on the name Lions to complement baseball's Detroit Tigers. In the Lions' first season in Detroit, team ownership instituted a long-standing tradition when they scheduled a game on Thanksgiving Day, which has featured a Lions' home game every year since (except during World War II).

In 1935 the Lions won their first NFL championship, behind the play of single-wing tailback Earl "Dutch" Clark. The team struggled throughout most of the 1940s, with only two winning seasons in the decade. The team's most notable player of this period was running back (and future U.S. Supreme Court justice) Byron R. "Whizzer" White, who played in Detroit from 1940 to 1941. Before the 1950 season, Detroit added quarterback Bobby Layne and running back Doak Walker—two future Hall of Famers—and the Lions became one of the better teams in the league by the following year. Detroit beat the Cleveland Browns in the NFL championship game in both 1952 and 1953, and the two teams faced off again in the 1953 championship, in which the Browns defeated the Lions. The Lions played the Browns for the NFL title a fourth time, in 1957, with Detroit handily beating Cleveland by 45 points to win its third championship in a six-year span.

The 1960s brought less success, as the team finished second in their division to the Green Bay Packers from 1960 to 1962 and missed the play-offs throughout the decade, despite a ferocious defense that featured defensive back Dick "Night Train" Lane, tackle Alex Karras, and linebackers Joe Schmidt and Wayne Walker. The Lions from this period are perhaps best remembered for writer George Plimpton's short tenure with the team as the "last-string" quarterback during the 1963 preseason, an experience recounted in his book *Paper Lion* (1966), which later was made into a movie of the same name.

Detroit qualified for only one play-off appearance in the 24 years from 1958 through 1981, though the team was often far from terrible, usually finishing their seasons with winning percentages around .500 during this prolonged period of mediocrity. In the early 1980s the Lions advanced to the postseason on two occasions, including a first-round loss to the Washington Redskins after posting only a 4–5 record in the strike-shortened 1982 season. Their 1983 play-off berth also ended with a loss in their first game, and the Lions dropped to the bottom of the divisional standings by the mid-1980s.

In 1989 the Lions drafted running back Barry Sanders, who would go on to earn Pro Bowl honours in each of his 10 seasons in the league, reinvigorating the franchise. The Lions lost to the Redskins in the 1991 NFC championship game, and they made it to the play-offs four additional times between 1992 and 1997. However, the Lions never advanced past their first postseason game in those seasons. In 2001 the team hired former NFL linebacker Matt Millen to serve as general manager, despite the fact that he had no previous front-office experience. Millen oversaw one of the most disastrous stretches for an NFL franchise of all time, as the Lions had a cumulative record of 31–84 during his tenure. He was met with a number of fan protests over his continued employment, and was fired early in the 2008 season, which saw the Lions post the first 0–16 season in league history.

GREEN BAY PACKERS

Based in Green Bay, Wis., the Packers have won the most championships, 12 in total, of any NFL team.

In 1919 Curly Lambeau and George Calhoun organized a group of men into a football team that soon managed a winning record against other amateur teams from Wisconsin, Michigan, and Minnesota. Lambeau, a shipping clerk for the Indian Packing Company, convinced his employer to donate money for the uniforms and, in the process, lent the nickname "Packers" to the team. In 1921, with Lambeau serving as head coach and playing halfback, the Packers entered the recently formed American Professional Football Association, which a year later would become the NFL. However, the team struggled with financial problems to the point of having to forfeit an entire season. In 1923 the team became a publicly owned nonprofit corporation supported by the people of Wisconsin and has remained so ever since.

Despite their rough financial start, the Packers won three consecutive championships from 1929 to 1931, with lineups that were laden with future Hall of Famers, including tackle Cal Hubbard, guard Mike Michalske, and halfback John "Blood" McNally. In 1935 the team added Don Hutson, who proceeded to redefine the wide receiver position and helped the Packers win championships in 1936, 1939, and 1944. Lambeau, who had stopped playing for the team in 1929, stepped away from head coaching duties in 1949, and the team struggled for wins throughout the next decade. The Packers posted a losing record seven times between 1950 and 1958.

The team's most successful period was in the 1960s under the legendary coach Vince Lombardi, who had been hired in 1959. Lombardi's Packer teams of the '60s were stocked with talent, boasting future Hall of Fame players on offense and defense: quarterback Bart Starr, fullback Jim Taylor, halfback Paul Hornung, tackle Forrest Gregg, linebacker Ray Nitschke, end Willie Davis, tackle Henry Jordan, cornerback Herb Adderley, and safety Willie Wood. They won championships in 1961 and 1962, and followed those titles with three straight championships starting in the 1965–66 season. On Jan. 15, 1967, in the inaugural Super Bowl, the Packers defeated the Kansas City Chiefs, 35–10. They successfully defended their Super Bowl title the following year against the Oakland Raiders, 33–14.

Lombardi left the Packers after their second Super Bowl championship, and Green Bay entered into a long period of relative futility, with just two play-off appearances in the 25 seasons from 1968 through 1992. Some of the team's scarce highlights during that period included the play of Hall of Fame wide receiver James Lofton, who starred for Green Bay from 1978 to 1986, and (ultimately unsuccessful) coaching stints by past Packers greats Starr and Gregg.

In 1992 the Packers brought in head coach Mike Holmgren and quarterback Brett Favre, who were the key pieces in the team's renaissance in the 1990s. Beginning in 1993, Green Bay qualified for the postseason in six straight years, including two NFC championships and subsequent trips to the Super Bowl. The team's third Super Bowl appearance, in 1997, was a success. They defeated the New England Patriots 35–21.

However, they did not repeat their win the following year against the Denver Broncos. After that loss Holmgren left the Packers for a job with the Seattle Seahawks. Favre

BART STARR

(b. Jan. 9, 1934, Montgomery, Ala., U.S.)

Quarterback Bart Starr led the Green Bay Packers to five league championships (1961–62, 1965–67) and to Super Bowl victories following the 1966 and 1967 seasons.

Bryan Bartlett Starr was quarterback for the University of Alabama (1952–55), completing 8 of 12 passes in the 1953 Orange Bowl victory over Syracuse and directing the team to a loss in the 1954 Cotton Bowl. He was drafted in the 17th round by the Packers in 1956 and played with them through the 1971 season. He became the team's starting quarterback in 1959, the first season Vince Lombardi coached the Packers.

A great leader and field tactician, Starr was particularly effective in postseason games: in six NFL title games, he completed 84 of 145 passes attempted for 1,090 yards, with only one interception. His performance in his two Super Bowl games was outstanding, and he was named Most Valuable Player in both of them. Four times All-NFL (1961–62, 1964, 1966), he led the league in percentage of passes completed four times (1962, 1966, and 1968–69) and average yards gained three times (1966–68). In 1964–65 he attempted 294 passes without interception, a record that survived until 1991.

After retiring as a player in 1972, Starr became head coach of the Packers from 1975 through 1983, yet his coaching success did not equal his success as a player. He was elected to the Pro Football Hall of Fame in 1977.

acrimoniously left the Packers in 2008, and the Packers' offense was given over to young star quarterback Aaron Rodgers. In 2011 Rodgers guided the sixth-seeded Packers to three postseason road victories, including a win over their longtime rival the Chicago Bears in the NFC championship game, to earn a berth in Super Bowl XLV against the Pittsburgh Steelers. The Packers proceeded to defeat the Steelers 31–26 to capture the franchise's fourth Super Bowl title.

From 1933 to 1994 the Packers elected to play some of their home games each year in Milwaukee to benefit from the larger market. Beginning in 1995, all home games were played at Lambeau Field in Green Bay, notwithstanding that city's small size (it did not exceed 100,000 residents until 2000) compared with virtually all other cities that have NFL franchises.

MINNESOTA VIKINGS

Based in Minneapolis, Minn., the Vikings have appeared in four Super Bowls (1970, 1974, 1975, 1977), losing each time.

Founded in 1961, the Vikings have a long and storied past, despite having won only one NFL championship, in 1969, the year before the AFL-NFL merger. The Vikings' most prominent period of success dates from the hiring of head coach Bud Grant in 1967. Grant, a future member of the Hall of Fame, guided the Vikings to all four of their Super Bowl appearances over the course of his career. His Vikings teams of the 1970s featured a tenacious defense line known as the "Purple People Eaters," which produced two Hall of Fame members (Alan Page and Carl Eller) and an efficient passing attack led by another future Hall of Fame member, quarterback Fran Tarkenton. Tarkenton paved the way for scrambling quarterbacks by being one of the first signal-callers to use his legs to make plays. The Vikings qualified for the play-offs in 10 of the 11 seasons between 1968 and 1978, but their 0–4 Super Bowl record is matched only by that of the Buffalo Bills teams of the 1990s.

The Vikings fell back into the NFL pack in the 1980s, a decade capped by a disastrous 1989 trade with the Dallas Cowboys that netted Minnesota underachieving running back Herschel Walker and gave Dallas draft choices that were used to select future NFL superstars Emmitt Smith and Darren Woodson, among others. The Vikings teams of the late 1990s and early 2000s featured an explosive offense, which starred running back Robert Smith and wide receivers Cris Carter and Randy Moss. The 1998 Vikings squad scored a then-NFL-record 556 points during the regular season on its way to a 15–1 record but was upset by the Atlanta Falcons in the NFC championship game.

In 2007 first-year running back Adrian Peterson, on his way to a Pro Bowl selection, set the record for most rushing yards in a single game, which provided a ray of hope for Minnesota's fans. The Vikings qualified for the play-offs in 2008 and, after adding quarterback Brett Favre in the offseason, did so again in 2009. Favre led the Vikings to the NFC championship game the following January, where the team lost a close contest to the New Orleans Saints.

NFC South

Atlanta Falcons

Based in Atlanta, the Falcons have played in one Super Bowl (1999), which they lost to the Denver Broncos.

The Falcons began play in 1966 as an expansion team, and they lost at least 11 of their 14 games in each of their first three seasons. The team slowly improved through the late 1960s and early '70s to post a 9–5 record in 1973 behind a defense led by linebacker Tommy Nobis and defensive end Claude Humphrey, narrowly missing out on a play-off spot in the process. Atlanta returned to the bottom of its division in 1974, and the team used the first pick of the 1975 NFL draft to select quarterback Steve

Bartkowski, who would go on to set franchise records in virtually every major passing category. Bartkowski led the Falcons to their first postseason berth in 1978, and in 1980 he teamed with running back William Andrews to form a high-powered offense that propelled Atlanta to its first division title. However, the Falcons lost in the first round of each of these postseasons, as well as during a third play-off appearance in the strike-shortened 1982 season. The franchise's play soon fell off; the team finished with double-digit losses in six of the seven seasons between 1984 and 1990.

A Falcons team featuring flashy personalities such as cornerback Deion Sanders, wide receiver Andre Rison, and flamboyant head coach Jerry Glanville won 10 games in 1991 but was again met with disappointment in the postseason. In 1998 the Falcons posted a club-best 14–2 record with a balanced team starring quarterback Chris Chandler and running back Jamal Anderson on offense and linebacker Jessie Tuggle on defense. The Falcons upset a 15–1 Minnesota Vikings team in the NFC championship game to earn their first Super Bowl berth against Denver.

The season after their Super Bowl loss to the Broncos, the Falcons plummeted to a 5–11 record. Atlanta had a few successful seasons in the mid-2000s with quarterback Michael Vick at the helm, which included the Falcons' handing the storied Green Bay Packers their first home play-off loss (in 2003) and the team's advancing to a second NFC championship game in 2005 (a loss to the Philadelphia Eagles). In 2008, led by first-year head coach Mike Smith, rookie quarterback Matt Ryan, and newly acquired running back Michael Turner, the Falcons qualified for the play-offs by adding seven wins to the previous year's total to compile an 11-5 record.

CAROLINA PANTHERS

Based in Charlotte, N.C., the Panthers represented the NFC in Super Bowl XXXVIII in 2004.

The Panthers played their first game in 1995, when they joined the Jacksonville Jaguars as the NFL's first expansion teams since 1976. Carolina became the most successful expansion franchise in league history when it won 7 of its 16 games in its inaugural season. The team further exceeded expectations the following year by winning 12 games, qualifying for the postseason, and advancing to the NFC championship game, in which it lost to the year's eventual Super Bowl champion, the Green Bay Packers. The Panthers were not able to capitalize on their startling early run, however, and they posted losing records in five of the next six years, including a disastrous one-win season in 2001 that led to the hiring of new team management and head coach John Fox.

Carolina's new leadership made a series of player acquisitions that quickly rebuilt the team into a contender. The Panthers drafted wide receiver Steve Smith and defensive tackle Kris Jenkins in 2001, and in 2002 they chose defensive end Julius Peppers with the draft's second overall selection. In addition, the Panthers signed quarterback Jake Delhomme before the 2003 season, and the team's revamped core led Carolina to an 11–5 record and a divisional championship the following season. In the play-offs, the Panthers beat the Dallas Cowboys, the St. Louis Rams, and the Philadelphia Eagles (the latter two on the road) to qualify for the Super Bowl in their second postseason appearance. In the Super Bowl, the Panthers lost a tight contest to the New England Patriots that was decided by a Patriots' field goal in the closing seconds of the game. Carolina remained one of the more consistently successful teams in the NFL over the remainder of the decade, with play-off appearances in 2005 and 2007.

NEW ORLEANS SAINTS

Based in New Orleans, the Saints have won one Super Bowl championship (2010).

The Saints began play in 1967 as an expansion franchise. Like most expansion teams, the Saints struggled in their first year in the NFL, losing 11 of their 14 games. However, the futility of the team's efforts was particularly pronounced, as it took 20 years for them to post their first winning season. Over those first decades the team garnered the somewhat affectionate nickname "The 'Aints" from their fans—some of whom attended home games at the Louisiana Superdome with bags over their heads in reaction to the franchise's prolonged ineffectiveness.

There were two notable figures to play for the Saints during that time. Archie Manning, the father of future NFL quarterbacks Peyton Manning and Eli Manning, was one of the most popular players in franchise history as quarterback of the team from 1971 to midway through the 1982 season. Tom Dempsey kicked an NFL-record (tied in 1998) 63-yard game-winning field goal in 1970, making him a fan favorite as well.

In 1983 the team's fans adopted a long-standing chant used at local high school and collegiate football games. The chant ("Who dat? Who dat? Who dat say dey gonna beat dem Saints?") is rooted in both Southern black folk culture and in the minstrel "adaptation" of it. The term "who dat" became a byname for the franchise among members of its fan base, who, in turn, began referring to themselves as the Who Dat Nation in the 21st century.

The Saints' first winning season came in 1987, as a high-scoring offense led by quarterback Bobby Hebert

Archie Manning warming up before playing a game with the New Orleans Saints. Focus On Sport/Getty Images

and a stout defense starring linebackers Rickey Jackson and Sam Mills combined to propel the Saints to a 12–3 record and a play-off berth. However, the Saints badly lost their first postseason contest to the Minnesota Vikings. New Orleans had winning records again in 1988 and 1989 but failed to appear in either postseason. In 1990 the team began a streak of three consecutive years of play-off berths and first-round postseason losses. An unexpected star of those play-offs was placekicker Morten Andersen, who was named to six Pro Bowls in his 13 seasons with the team (1982–94) and would later go on to set the NFL record for most career points scored.

New Orleans soon returned to mediocrity, losing at least 10 games in each season between 1996 and 1999. The Saints had a surprising turnaround in 2000, however, winning 10 games to qualify for the postseason and defeating the reigning Super Bowl champion St. Louis Rams for the franchise's first play-off victory. Then the postseason eluded the Saints for the following five years.

The team's return to the play-offs in 2006 was especially notable. Having been forced to play all their 2005 "home" games outside New Orleans because of the damage caused by Hurricane Katrina, the Saints came back to the Superdome in 2006 and posted a 10–6 record under first-year head coach Sean Payton. Featuring a potent offense led by quarterback Drew Brees, the Saints became national media darlings as they rebounded from the previous season's adversity and defeated the Philadelphia Eagles in the postseason en route to their first NFC championship game, which they lost to the Chicago Bears.

In 2009 the Saints won their first 13 games of the season and qualified for the play-offs as the NFC's highest-seeded team. In the postseason they defeated the Arizona Cardinals and the Minnesota Vikings en route to

DREW BREES

(b. Jan. 15, 1979, Dallas, Texas, U.S.)

Drew Brees is best known for leading the New Orleans Saints to the team's first Super Bowl championship, in 2010.

Brees was a standout high school football player in Austin, Texas, leading his team to a state title and taking Texas 5A (the division that features the state's largest high schools) Offensive Player of the Year honours in 1996. Considered too short (standing 6 feet [1.83 metres] tall) and too weak-armed by the major college programs in his home state, he attended Purdue University in West Lafayette, Ind. Brees was a three-year starter at Purdue, where he set school and Big Ten Conference records for almost every major career passing statistic, including passing yards and touchdowns. In his senior season he led the Purdue Boilermakers to their first Rose Bowl berth in 34 years and finished third in the voting for the Heisman Trophy, college football's highest individual honour.

Brees was selected by the San Diego Chargers with the first pick of the second round of the 2001 NFL draft. He became the team's starting quarterback in his second season, but he failed to quickly turn around the then-woeful Chargers and in his third year lost playing time to 41-year-old Doug Flutie. When the Chargers acquired promising rookie quarterback Philip Rivers in 2004, it was assumed that Brees's days in San Diego were numbered. Brees, however, remained the Chargers' starting quarterback during the 2004 season and led the team to a surprising 12–4 record en route to earning the NFL's Comeback Player of the Year award and Pro Bowl honours. He followed this with a solid if unspectacular season in 2005, but a shoulder injury in the season finale made the Chargers wary of signing him to a long-term contract, and Brees instead signed a free agent deal with the Saints.

In his first year in New Orleans, Brees reversed the fortunes of a team that had gone 3–13 the previous season, leading the Saints to a 10–6 record in 2006 and a berth in the NFC championship game. He led the league in passing yards that year and was named first-team All-Pro for his efforts. In 2008 Brees threw for 5,069 yards — 15 fewer than Dan Marino's single-season record — and was once again voted to the Pro Bowl. In 2009 Brees had another Pro Bowl season and set an NFL record by completing 70.6 percent of his passes. More significantly, he led the Saints to a franchise-best 13–0 start and the franchise's first Super Bowl berth, a victory over the Indianapolis Colts. In the Super Bowl, Brees completed 32 passes (which tied Tom Brady's Super Bowl record) for 288 yards and two touchdowns, and he was named the game's Most Valuable Player.

the Saints' first Super Bowl appearance, a victory over the Indianapolis Colts in Super Bowl XLIV.

Tampa Bay Buccaneers

Based in Tampa, Fla., the Buccaneers won a Super Bowl title in 2003.

The Buccaneers (often shortened to "Bucs") were established in 1976, and they posted an ignoble 0–14 record in their initial season in the NFL. After playing their first season in the AFC, the Bucs moved to their current conference in 1977. The team's losing ways continued in the NFC, as Tampa Bay did not record the first win in franchise history until December 1977; their 26-game losing streak remains an NFL record. These early Buccaneer teams were notable for the presence of future Hall of Fame defensive end Lee Roy Selmon and for their charismatic head coach John McKay, whose many quips about the team's failures endeared him to football fans nationwide.

In 1979, led by quarterback Doug Williams, the Bucs — to the surprise of many observers—won 10 games and qualified for the postseason. They advanced to the conference championship game but lost to the Los Angeles Rams. Tampa Bay went on to play-off berths in 1981 and 1982 before falling back to the bottom of the conference standings with a 2–14 record in 1983.

The 1983 campaign began a dubious streak of 12 consecutive seasons that saw the Buccaneers post double-digit loss totals. Over that period, the team also had an unfortunate penchant for acquiring many high-profile players—including running back Bo Jackson and quarterbacks Steve Young and Vinny Testaverde—who would play poorly (or not at all) in Tampa Bay, only to go on to have great success with other teams.

The franchise's fortunes began to turn around in the late 1990s as head coach Tony Dungy built one of the best defenses in the NFL, featuring tackle Warren Sapp, linebacker Derrick Brooks, and defensive backs John Lynch and Ronde Barber. The Bucs made four postseason appearances in the five seasons from 1997 through 2001, but the offensively limited team scored fewer than 10 points in each of their four play-off losses in that span. Dungy was fired in early 2002 despite his regular-season success.

The Buccaneers hired head coach Jon Gruden to improve the team's offense, but it was the top-ranked defense in the league that helped the team post a 12–4 record in 2002 (which was tied for the best mark in the NFL) and upset the Philadelphia Eagles in the NFC championship game the following January. At Super Bowl XXXVII, the Bucs soundly defeated the Oakland Raiders 48–21 to capture their first championship. The Bucs missed out on the postseason the following two years but returned to the play-offs after the 2005 and 2007 seasons, both of which ended in opening-round losses at home. A late-season collapse by the team in 2008—the Bucs lost four consecutive games to close out the season after starting the year 9–3—led to the firing of Gruden and a massive coaching, management, and roster turnover in an attempt to rebuild the franchise from the ground up.

NFC West

Arizona Cardinals

Based in Phoenix, the Cardinals are the oldest team in the NFL, but they are also one of the least successful franchises in league history, having won just two NFL championships (1925, 1947) since the team's founding in 1898.

The Cardinals started out as the Morgan Athletic Club, a neighbourhood team based in the South Side of Chicago. The team acquired its nickname in 1901 when its founder, Chris O'Brien, received a shipment of faded jerseys from the University of Chicago Maroons football team that were cardinal red in colour. Known as the Racine Cardinals, after the name of the Chicago street on which the team's playing field was located, the team played in a loosely organized "league" composed of Chicago-area amateur clubs.

The Cardinals' continued success and popularity gave the team the opportunity to join the American Professional Football League (the forerunner of the NFL) when it was founded in 1920. The team was renamed the Chicago Cardinals in 1922 when a franchise from Racine, Wis., joined the NFL. Three years later the Cardinals were credited with their first NFL championship after compiling a record of 11 wins, two losses, and one tie over the course of the 1925 season.

After 1925 the team entered into a long stretch of noncompetitive and sometimes dismal years, which included consecutive 0–10 seasons in 1943 and 1944. Having already coached the team from 1940 to 1942, Jimmy Conzelman was rehired in 1946. Conzelman oversaw a Cardinals victory in the 1947 NFL championship game behind the play of the team's famed "Million-Dollar Backfield." This feat was followed by a franchise-best 11–1 record and another trip to the title game in 1948, where the Cardinals fell to the Philadelphia Eagles, 7–0.

Conzelman left the team the next year, and the Cardinals embarked on another extended period of poor play. This led to a decline in revenue, and in 1960 the franchise relocated to St. Louis, Mo., where the team was invariably referred to as the St. Louis "football" Cardinals, in deference to the city's beloved Major League Baseball team of the same name.

The Cardinals began posting winning records more frequently in St. Louis, but the postseason evaded them until 1974, when a team featuring quarterback Jim Hart, running back Terry Metcalf, and a pair of future Hall of Famers, offensive lineman Dan Dierdorf and tight end Jackie Smith, won 10 games and made the first of two consecutive trips to the play-offs, where they lost each time. The Cardinals returned to the play-offs again during the strike-shortened 1982 season, but a general lack of fan support—combined with the ownership's desire for a profitable home stadium—induced the team to move to Phoenix in 1988.

The Cardinals' mediocre play continued until 1998, when quarterback Jake Plummer led the team to a nine-win season and its first play-off victory in 51 years. The team's momentum did not continue on into the next year, and yet another long play-off drought ensued. In 2008 the Cardinals had their most successful season since their relocation to Arizona, as veteran quarterback Kurt Warner, heading a powerful offense highlighted by Pro Bowl wide receivers Larry Fitzgerald and Anquan Boldin, guided the team to a division title and the franchise's first Super Bowl appearance the following February, where they lost to the Pittsburgh Steelers.

St. Louis Rams

Based in St. Louis, Mo., the Rams have won two NFL championships (1945, 1951) and one Super Bowl (2000).

The Rams began play in 1936 as a member of the short-lived AFL (they joined the NFL the following year) and were originally located in Cleveland. The new team lost all but one game in its first season in the NFL and failed to post a winning season in any of the following five seasons. The Rams had to suspend operations in 1943 due to a player shortage caused by World War II. In 1945 rookie quarterback Bob Waterfield led the Rams to their first winning season (9–1) and a victory over the Washington Redskins in the NFL championship game. The 1945 championship game would prove to be the Rams' final game in Cleveland, as team owner Dan Reeves moved the franchise to Los Angeles in 1946 rather than compete with the new Cleveland Browns franchise of the All-America Football Conference. In 1948 the Rams became the first professional football team to add an insignia (a pair of golden ram's horns) to their helmets, an innovation that would pay great dividends for the sport as it entered into the television era, when iconic helmets helped teams create salient identities among football fans.

In the early 1950s the Rams featured high-powered offense starring quarterback Norm Van Brocklin and ends Elroy Hirsch and Tom Fears, all future Hall of Famers. The team posted no losing seasons between 1950 and 1955, defeating the Browns to win the 1951 NFL championship. The Rams' success helped the team set attendance records through the end of the 1950s and into the next decade.

In the 1960s the team was defined by a standout defensive line nicknamed "The Fearsome Foursome": tackles Merlin Olsen and Roosevelt "Rosie" Grier and ends Deacon Jones and Lamar Lundy. The Rams also featured

DEACON JONES

(b. Dec. 9, 1938, Eatonville, Fla., U.S.)

Defensive end Deacon Jones is regarded as one of the sport's premier defense players.

David D. Jones, an accomplished high school athlete in Orlando, Fla., played football at South Carolina State College and Mississippi Vocational College. He was relatively unknown in 1961, when the Los Angeles Rams selected him in the 14th round of the NFL draft, but he soon distinguished himself as the left defensive end of the Rams' "Fearsome Foursome," the moniker of the team's renowned defensive line.

Jones was surprisingly agile for his powerful frame—about 6 feet 5 inches (1.9 m) and 250 pounds (113 kg)—and he was praised for his ability to pursue a ballcarrier from sideline to sideline. The outspoken Jones coined the term "sack" for the act of tackling the quarterback behind the line of scrimmage, a facet of the game at which he excelled. He also popularized the head slap, a move (since banned) that involved a defensive player slapping an offensive lineman's helmet as hard as he could at the snap in order to stun the blocker and thus gain an advantage off of the line. He was named All-Pro five consecutive times (1965–69) and the NFL Defensive Player of the Year twice, in 1967 and 1968.

Jones left the Rams in 1972 to play two seasons with the San Diego Chargers, before playing his final year with the Washington Redskins in 1974. During his 14-year professional career, he missed only five regular-season games and was named to eight Pro Bowls. Both during his playing days and after his retirement, Jones dabbled in acting and singing, and in his later years he remained in the public eye through frequent appearances on television programs about the history of football, which highlighted his colourful personality. He was enshrined in the Pro Football Hall of Fame in 1980 and in 1994 was named to the NFL's 75th Anniversary All-Time Team.

pro football's first "big" quarterback, 6 feet 5 inches (1.9-metre) Roman Gabriel. As dominant as the Foursome was, however, the Rams never advanced any further than the divisional play-off round over the course of the '60s.

The team made a club-record eight consecutive play-off berths from 1973 to 1980, led by a formidable defensive unit that starred defensive end Jack Youngblood. During this streak, the Rams recorded at least 10 wins in a season on seven occasions, and they reached the NFC championship game five times, winning just once. That victory came following the 1979 regular season, during which the Rams went just 9–7 before embarking on a play-off run that saw the team win two consecutive road games before ultimately losing to the Pittsburgh Steelers in Super Bowl XIV. In the 1980s the team was notable for featuring a rushing attack that was led by offensive lineman Jackie Slater and running back Eric Dickerson. The Rams were largely successful during the decade—failing to qualify for the play-offs just three times in those 10 years—but they failed to return to the Super Bowl.

In the early 1990s the team's lack of on-field success (the Rams won no more than six games in each season between 1990 and 1994) and the resultant decline in attendance, in addition to owner Georgia Frontiere's desire to play in a more profitable stadium, led Frontiere to begin casting about for new homes for the Rams. In 1995 the team received approval from the NFL to move to St. Louis, and, in a reversal of a decades-long trend in sports franchise relocations, the Rams became the first professional football team to leave the West Coast.

The Rams' initial seasons in St. Louis were inauspicious, as their victory total declined in each of their first four years in their new home, culminating in a dismal 1998 campaign that saw the team go 4–12. In 1999 the Rams embarked on one of the most remarkable turnarounds in league history. Behind unheralded former backup quarterback Kurt Warner, who led a potent offense that was later nicknamed "The Greatest Show on Turf," featuring running back Marshall Faulk as well as wide receivers Isaac

Bruce and Torry Holt, the Rams went 13–3 in the 1999 regular season and advanced to the second Super Bowl in franchise history. There the team won a thrilling victory over the Tennessee Titans, 23–16, to capture its first Super Bowl title. The Rams continued to be one of the highest-scoring teams in the league through the first years of the 21st century and returned once more to the Super Bowl in 2002 but lost to the New England Patriots. As the members of the Greatest Show on Turf departed, the team's play declined, and the Rams closed out the first decade of the 2000s as one of the worst teams in the NFL.

SAN FRANCISCO 49ERS

Based in San Francisco, the 49ers have won five Super Bowl titles and five NFC championships (1982, 1985, 1989, 1990, and 1995).

The San Francisco 49ers were established in the All-America Football Conference (AAFC) in 1946. The team had a winning record in each of its first four years, but it could not displace the dominant Cleveland Browns, who won every championship in the four seasons of the AAFC. After the AAFC merged with the NFL in 1950, the 49ers struggled through their first losing season. Despite the presence of five future Hall of Famers—quarterback Y.A. Tittle, running backs Hugh McElhenny and Joe Perry, tackle Bob St. Clair, and defensive lineman Leo Nomellini—the 49ers were mostly unsuccessful during the 1950s, advancing to the postseason only once, in 1957. San Francisco began a string of 12 consecutive seasons without a play-off berth in 1958. One of the most noteworthy players on the team during the 1960s was running back Dave Kopay, who in 1977 became the first athlete from a major American team sport to publicly acknowledge that he was a homosexual. A resurgent 49ers squad under the guidance of head coach Dick Nolan and led by quarterback John Brodie advanced to the NFC championship game in both 1971 and 1972 but lost to the Dallas Cowboys on both occasions.

The 49ers ascendancy began in 1979, when quarterback Joe Montana was drafted by new head coach Bill Walsh. Upon his arrival in San Francisco, Walsh installed his innovative "West Coast offense," which relied on a series of quick, accurate passes and was a perfect fit for Montana's skills. San Francisco rebounded from a 2–14 record in Walsh's first year to the franchise's first Super Bowl win in his third. The 49ers' title run was highlighted by a last-second victory over the Cowboys in the NFC championship game off a brilliant touchdown pass from Montana to wide receiver Dwight Clark, which was immortalized as "The Catch."

The 49ers lost to the Washington Redskins in the 1984 NFC championship game, but they lost only one game the following year and returned to the Super Bowl, where they easily defeated the Miami Dolphins. In the 1985 NFL draft, the team selected wide receiver Jerry Rice, who would team with Montana to create one of the most prolific passing duos in NFL history on his way to breaking every major career receiving record. After guiding the 49ers to a third Super Bowl win in 1989, Walsh retired and handed head-coaching duties to his defensive coordinator George Seifert.

While the 49ers teams of the 1980s were best known for their offensive prowess, their defense featured a number of star players, including future Hall of Fame safety Ronnie Lott. San Francisco's dominance on both sides of the ball was evidenced in 1990, when the 49ers defeated the Denver Broncos 55–10 in the most lopsided Super Bowl victory of all time. An injury to Montana in 1991 gave Steve Young an opportunity to step in as the 49ers' starting quarterback. Young excelled in his new role, which

BILL WALSH

(b. Nov. 30, 1931, Los Angeles, Calif., U.S.—d. July 30, 2007, Woodside, Calif.)

Bill Walsh was an influential football coach, whose "West Coast offense" changed pro football during the 1980s. Among his most celebrated players were quarterback Joe Montana and receiver Jerry Rice, holder of nearly every professional pass-catching record.

Although only an average athlete, William Ernest Walsh entered coaching upon his graduation from San Jose State in 1955. He coached on the high school, junior college, and college level before becoming an assistant coach for the Cincinnati Bengals of the NFL in 1968. There he served as end and quarterback coach under Paul Brown through 1975, earning praise for developing Ken Anderson into a star quarterback.

When Brown retired, Walsh was disappointed not to be named his successor. He briefly considered retiring from coaching. Instead, he joined the San Diego Chargers' staff, where he was credited with turning Dan Fouts into a Hall of Fame quarterback. In two seasons (1977–78) as head coach at Stanford University (Calif.), he led the team to two victories in bowl games.

In 1979 Walsh returned to the NFL as head coach of the San Francisco 49ers. The team struggled to a 2–14–0 record in his first season but by 1981 had emerged as NFL champions with a victory in Super Bowl XVI. Under Walsh the 49ers also won Super Bowls XIX (1985) and XXIII (1989) and registered a record of 102–63–1. After retiring in 1989, he worked as a television analyst before returning in 1992 to Stanford, where he coached for three seasons. Walsh later served as a consultant to the 49ers and held several other posts with the team.

Walsh believed in "scripting"—selecting ahead of time—the first 25 plays of a game. His "West Coast offense" was a ball-control offense that featured short passes and quick slanting pass routes by receivers and running backs. This resulted in coverage mismatches and space for the backs and receivers to break long runs. Walsh was inducted into the Pro Football Hall of Fame in 1993.

allowed the 49ers to trade Montana in 1993, and the team won a fifth Super Bowl in 1995. Young's retirement in 1999 marked a symbolic end to the 49ers long reign atop the NFL—the team had qualified for the postseason in 15 of the 16 seasons between 1983 and 1998 — and San Francisco has struggled to field a consistently competitive team in recent seasons.

SEATTLE SEAHAWKS

Based in Seattle, the Seahawks are the only NFL team to have played in both the AFC and NFC championship games.

Along with fellow expansion team the Tampa Bay Buccaneers, the Seahawks began play in 1976. After an initial season in the NFC followed by a move to the AFC in 1977, the Seahawks recorded their first winning season in 1978, earning head coach Jack Patera NFL Coach of the Year honours. The early Seahawks teams were led by quarterback Jim Zorn, running back Curt Warner, and wide receiver Steve Largent, who retired as the NFL's all-time leading receiver and in 1995 was the first Seahawk inducted into the Pro Football Hall of Fame. In 1983 head coach Chuck Knox led the Seahawks to the AFC championship game in his first season with the team, and over the next nine years he posted a record of 83 wins and 67 losses. The Seahawks had their worst season in franchise history after Knox left in 1991, winning only two games that season. The following years saw many seasons of on-field struggle as well as off-field controversy, as team majority owner Ken Behring announced plans to move the team to Los Angeles in 1996, citing as the reason the condition of the team's home stadium, the Kingdome.

In 1997 billionaire Microsoft cofounder Paul Allen purchased the Seahawks and helped push through public funding for a new football stadium, which kept the team in Seattle. Allen hired Mike Holmgren as head coach and general manager in 1999. In 2000 the team drafted running back Shaun Alexander and the following year traded for quarterback Matt Hasselbeck, who, along with All-Pro offensive lineman Walter Jones, formed the core of the most successful team in Seahawks history. After 25 seasons playing in the AFC, the Seahawks moved to the NFC in 2002 as part of an NFL realignment. The Seahawks made the play-offs in five of their first six seasons in the NFC. In 2006 the franchise made its first trip to the Super Bowl, which the team lost to the Pittsburgh Steelers. Seattle's play fell off after 2007, and—after Holmgren left the Seahawks following the 2008 season—the team made a series of front-office, coaching, and player personnel changes in an effort to rebuild.

In 2011 the Seahawks became the first team in NFL history with a losing record—after going 7–9 in the 2010 regular season—to qualify for the play-offs. After upsetting the defending champion New Orleans Saints, Seattle was eliminated in the second round of postseason play by the Chicago Bears.

THE AMERICAN FOOTBALL CONFERENCE (AFC)

AFC EAST

BUFFALO BILLS

Based in Buffalo, the Bills won two AFL championships (1964, 1965), and they appeared in a record four consecutive Super Bowls (1991–94), losing on each occasion.

The Bills were one of the eight founding members of the AFL (1960). They were one of the worst teams in the league in their first two seasons, but the addition of quarterback Jack Kemp and punishing running back Cookie Gilchrist during the 1962 season helped turn around the franchise's fortunes. That year Gilchrist was named the AFL's Most Valuable Player, and the next he set a league record by rushing for 243 yards in a game. In 1963, his first full season with the team, Kemp guided the Bills to a play-off appearance. The following year the Bills won 12 of their 14 games and finished with the AFL's highest-ranked offense and defense. To cap off the season, Buffalo defeated the San Diego Chargers to win its first championship in only its fifth year of existence. The Bills repeated their title-game victory over the Chargers in 1965, and in 1966 they again returned to the AFL championship game, only to lose to the Kansas City Chiefs and be denied entry into the inaugural AFL-NFL World Championship Game (now called the Super Bowl).

Buffalo then entered into a prolonged period of losing seasons, including a league-worst 1–12–1 record in 1968 that gave the team the first selection in the 1969 NFL draft (the two leagues held a joint draft for three years before their merger in 1970), which it used to select running back O.J. Simpson. Running behind a powerful offensive line known as "The Electric Company"—because they "turned on the Juice," an allusion to Simpson's nickname—Simpson set a number of NFL rushing records in his nine years with the Bills, including having the league's first 2,000-yard rushing season in 1973. Yet the team advanced to the play-offs only once over that span. The Bills continued to struggle for a few seasons after Simpson was traded to the San Francisco 49ers in 1978, but in 1980 they made their first of two consecutive postseason berths.

The Bills drafted quarterback Jim Kelly in the first round of the 1983 NFL draft. Kelly instead signed to play in the upstart United States Football League (USFL), and Buffalo posted league-worst 2–14 records in both 1984 and 1985. After the USFL folded in 1986, Kelly joined the Bills, who had retained his NFL rights. Head coach Marv Levy soon took advantage of his quarterback's skill set and instituted a no-huddle "K-Gun" offense (named after Kelly), which was based on a series of fast-paced passes and runs out of the shotgun formation. The Buffalo offense, which also featured future Hall of Fame running back Thurman Thomas and perennial Pro Bowl receiver Andre Reed, was one of the most prolific in the league at this time; the team's defense was anchored by all-time great defensive end Bruce Smith and star linebacker Cornelius Bennett. Between 1988 and 1993, the Bills made six straight play-off appearances, winning five division titles.

The team had a number of notable postseason exploits over those years. The Bills advanced to their first Super Bowl in 1991, which they lost to the New York Giants after a last-second field goal attempt by Buffalo's Scott Norwood missed wide right. The next year Buffalo returned to the Super Bowl, where it was defeated by the Washington Redskins. In the 1992 postseason's Wild Card round, the Bills—playing without an injured Kelly—trailed the Houston Oilers by a score of 35–3 early in the third quarter. Backup quarterback Frank Reich rallied the Bills to five unanswered touchdowns, and Buffalo prevailed over the Oilers 41–38 in overtime. The Bills' feat was the greatest point-differential comeback in NFL history, including both regular-season and postseason games.

The team's momentum continued throughout the AFC play-offs, and the Bills easily won two road games to advance to a third Super Bowl. There, however, they were soundly defeated by the Dallas Cowboys 52–17. Buffalo made it to a record fourth consecutive Super Bowl in 1994, but its rematch against the Cowboys ended in another disappointing loss in the big game. The Bills made two more postseason appearances in the mid-1990s but failed to advance past the second round of the play-offs each time. The key members of the team's 1990s dynasty all soon retired.

Quarterback Doug Flutie led the Bills to brief postseason berths after both the 1998 and 1999 seasons, but the franchise fell back to the middle of the AFC standings in the 2000s. The financially struggling team was dogged by rumours of an impending move to Toronto, which only increased when the Bills agreed to play eight games (including both preseason and regular-season contests) in the Canadian city between 2008 and 2012.

MIAMI DOLPHINS

Based in Miami, the Dolphins have had a rich history that has included two Super Bowl championships (1973–74) and five conference titles. The Dolphins are the only team in NFL history to finish an entire season undefeated; their 1972 season ended without a loss and culminated in a victory in Super Bowl VII.

The Dolphins joined the AFL in 1966. Failures during the team's infancy brought about the hiring of head coach Don Shula from the Baltimore Colts in 1970, shortly after the merger of the AFL and the NFL. Shula immediately turned the Dolphins around and led them to play-off appearances in each of his first five seasons with the team, including the Dolphins' first trip to the Super Bowl in January 1972, which they lost to the Dallas Cowboys. Featuring the "no-name" defense, captained by middle linebacker Nick Buoniconti, and a potent offense led by five players destined for the Hall of Fame—quarterback Bob Griese (who was injured mid-season and replaced by Earl Morrall), wide receiver Paul Warfield, running back Larry Csonka, and linemen Larry Little and Jim Langer—the 1972 Dolphins team dominated the NFL en route to posting the only undefeated season in league history. Returning to the Super Bowl the following season and thus becoming the first franchise to make three consecutive Super Bowl appearances, Miami beat the Minnesota Vikings 24–7. The Dolphins often fielded competitive teams throughout the remainder of

LARRY CSONKA

(b. Dec. 25, 1946, Stow, Ohio, U.S.)

Powerful running back Larry Csonka won two Super Bowls (1973, 1974) playing for the Miami Dolphins and was named Most Valuable Player of Super Bowl VIII.

Lawrence Richard Csonka was an All-American fullback at Syracuse University, where he was noted for his straight-ahead power. He was chosen by the Dolphins with the eighth selection of the 1968 NFL draft, and he was immediately thrust into the team's starting lineup. In each of three consecutive years (1971–73) he rushed for more than 1,000 yards, and in 1972 he was a mainstay in the Dolphin's perfect 17–0 season. After moving to the short-lived World Football League in 1975, Csonka returned to the NFL to play for the New York Giants from 1976 to 1978 before finishing his career with the Dolphins in 1979. Csonka was inducted into the Pro Football Hall of Fame in 1987.

the 1970s, but they did not appear in another Super Bowl during the decade.

In 1983 the Dolphins drafted quarterback Dan Marino, who would go on to set major career NFL passing records and be inducted into the Pro Football Hall of Fame. Teamed with the "Marks Brothers"—wide receivers Mark Clayton and Mark Duper—and working behind a line anchored by centre Dwight Stephenson, Marino ran an offense that often ranked at the top of the league. Despite experiencing a great deal of regular-season success, Marino and the Dolphins advanced to the Super Bowl only once in his 17-year career, a 38–16 loss to the San Francisco 49ers in 1985.

Subsequent history was not kind to the Dolphins. Defensive-minded squads led by defensive end Jason Taylor, linebacker Zach Thomas, and cornerback Sam Madison experienced moderate success beginning in the late 1990s, but in 2002 the team entered into the longest postseason drought in franchise history. A disastrous one-win season in 2007 prompted the hiring of Super Bowl–winning coach Bill Parcells as head of football operations, bringing hope for a return to form. Miami posted 11 wins and 5 losses in 2008 (which tied the NFL record for the greatest win improvement from the previous season) and won a division championship.

New England Patriots

Based in Foxborough, Mass., the Patriots have won three Super Bowl titles (2002, 2004, 2005) and six AFC championships.

The franchise joined the AFL in 1960 as the Boston Patriots and quickly fielded a competitive team that featured quarterback Vito "Babe" Parilli, linebacker Nick Buoniconti, and wide receiver Gino Cappelletti. The Patriots posted a winning record in their second season and advanced to the AFL championship game in their fourth. However, after a second place divisional finish in 1966, the team recorded seven consecutive losing seasons. The Patriots also struggled to find a permanent home stadium, playing at four different Boston-area locations in 10 years. In 1971 the team—a member of the NFL following the 1970 AFL-NFL merger—relocated to Foxborough and was renamed the New England Patriots.

Led by John Hannah, considered one of the greatest offensive linemen in NFL history, future Hall of Fame cornerback Mike Haynes, and quarterback Steve Grogan, the Patriots experienced sporadic success in the 1970s and '80s. They advanced to their first Super Bowl in 1986 but lost to a dominant Chicago Bears team, 46–10. Eleven years would pass before the Patriots would return to the Super Bowl, this time under the direction of coach Bill Parcells and led by quarterback Drew Bledsoe. New England lost Super Bowl XXXI to the Green Bay Packers, but their postseason appearance marked the beginning of three straight years of play-off football for the team, then a franchise record.

The Patriots made one of the most significant moves in franchise history with the hiring of Bill Belichick as head coach in 2000. A noted defensive assistant coach through most of his career (he also had a stint as the head coach of the Cleveland Browns, 1991–95), Belichick quickly built a powerful team around unheralded veteran free agents (such as linebacker Mike Vrabel and running back Corey Dillon) and savvy draft picks (including linebacker Tedy Bruschi and cornerback Ty Law). In 2001 a serious injury to Bledsoe paved the way for Tom Brady, a relatively unknown sixth-round draft choice, to take over the Patriots' offense and lead the team to a surprising Super Bowl win the following February. Brady would become an elite passer and guide the Patriots to two more Super Bowl victories in 2004 and 2005.

New England traded for All-Pro wide receiver Randy Moss before the 2007 season and went on to shatter numerous offensive records and post the only 16–0 regular-season record in NFL history, only to lose to the underdog New York Giants in Super Bowl XLII. The Patriots posted the best record in the NFL during the 2010 regular season, but lost to the New York Jets in their opening play-off game the following January.

NEW YORK JETS

Based in Florham Park, N.J., the Jets, behind the play of future Hall of Fame quarterback Joe Namath, won a historic upset in the 1969 Super Bowl over the Baltimore Colts. The Jets share a home stadium with the New York Giants in East Rutherford, N.J.

Established as one of the founding teams of the upstart AFL in 1960, the franchise—known as the Titans until 1963—was marred by financial struggles and athletic mediocrity as the team competed with the older Giants franchise in the New York market. One of the lone bright spots in the team's early years was wide receiver Don Maynard, who joined the team in its inaugural season and would set most major receiving records during the course of his Hall of Fame career. In 1963 the newly renamed Jets hired head coach Weeb Ewbank (who had guided the Colts to championships in the late 1950s) and in 1965 acquired Joe Namath, which marked the beginning of the team's move to respectability. Known as "Broadway Joe," the famed quarterback's good looks and late-night partying won him both adoring fans and commercial endorsements.

Namath's swagger was most memorably on display when, in the week before the 1969 Super Bowl, he guaranteed a victory over the heavily favoured Colts of the NFL, which was widely considered to be the superior professional football league and had easily taken the first two Super Bowls. Namath made good on his promise as the Jets defeated the Colts, 16–7. The Jets' victory showed that the two leagues were on an equal footing, helping to ease owners' concerns prior to the 1970 AFL-NFL merger.

Namath was waived in 1977 after a long play-off drought that began in 1970. Led by a fierce defensive line nicknamed the "New York Sack Exchange," the Jets returned to the postseason in 1981 and advanced to the AFC championship game the following year. The Jets were intermittently successful throughout the remainder of the 1980s and the early 1990s, but the team experienced its greatest extended period of success beginning in 1998. That season ended with the Jets, led by coach Bill Parcells (who had earlier led the New York Giants to two

JOE NAMATH

(b. May 31, 1943, Beaver Falls, Penn., U.S.)

Joe Namath was one of the best passers in football and a cultural sports icon of the 1960s.

Joseph William Namath excelled in several sports as a youth in the steel-mill town of Beaver Falls, near Pittsburgh. He played football at the University of Alabama (1962–64) under coach Bear Bryant, a famous developer of quarterbacks. While playing in college, he sustained the first of many knee injuries that ultimately shortened his career. The NFL and the AFL competed for him as a first-round draft choice, and he went to the AFL New York Jets with an unprecedented three-year contract for more than $400,000. He became the Jets' starting quarterback midway through his first season, and in 1967 he threw for a record 4,007 yards.

Like the boxer Muhammad Ali, Namath represented a transformation of the American sports hero in the 1960s. Namath was known as much for his late-night carousing with beautiful women as for his performances on the field. He was the new kind of ideal male, defined by his countercultural style, which included modish long hair that hung below his helmet and white football shoes (when everyone else wore black). His masculinity was so unquestionable that he posed in panty hose for a magazine advertisement. And at a time when athletes were expected to be modest and self-deprecating, Namath "guaranteed" that the Jets would defeat the favoured NFL Baltimore Colts in the 1969 Super Bowl; they did, 16–7.

In 1969 Namath retired briefly over the issue of his ownership of a New York City nightclub (hence his nickname "Broadway Joe"), but he sold it and returned to the Jets. In the same year, he was chosen for the all-time AFL team (the AFL and the NFL merged in 1970). As players throughout the league adopted Namath's personal style, his own career played out anticlimactically. He played with the Jets through the 1976 season, sustaining further injuries, but he had by then set seasonal and career records for most games with 300 yards or more gained by passing. In 1977–78 he was a backup quarterback for the Los Angeles Rams, after which he retired. He was inducted into the Pro Football Hall of Fame in 1985.

He remained in the public eye through television commercials and film, television, and theatre appearances.

Super Bowl victories) and featuring running back Curtis Martin and wide receiver Keyshawn Johnson, losing to the Denver Broncos in the 1999 AFC championship game. The Jets qualified for the play-offs in four of the following eight seasons, but they never truly contended in the highly competitive AFC.

In the summer of 2008 the Jets traded for former Green Bay Packers quarterback Brett Favre in hopes of improving the club's fortunes, but after a 9–7 season, which was not good enough to qualify the team for the postseason, Favre left the Jets and a new coaching regime was brought in. In 2009, under new head coach Rex Ryan, the Jets repeated their 9–7 record from the previous season but this time advanced to the play-offs, where they won two road contests before ultimately falling to the Indianapolis Colts in the AFC championship game.

The following season the Jets again posted two road wins in the first rounds of the play-offs, against the Indianapolis Colts and the New England Patriots, but lost to the Pittsburgh Steelers in the AFC championship game.

AFC North

Baltimore Ravens

Based in Baltimore, Md., the Ravens are a relatively young franchise, having played their first game in 1996. The Ravens nevertheless won a Super Bowl title in 2001.

The Ravens originated when Cleveland Browns owner Art Modell decided to relocate his historic franchise, and he reached a deal with the city of Baltimore to move his team in 1996. As part of the agreement, Cleveland kept the Browns' name, history, and colours for a future replacement team, so the newly renamed Ravens—the moniker stems from the famous poem by Baltimorean Edgar Allan

THE BRITANNICA GUIDE TO FOOTBALL

Poe—were technically an expansion team. The franchise's first draft selection was linebacker Ray Lewis, who quickly became one of the most dominant players in the NFL and helped forge the Ravens' reputation as a team known for its ferocious defense.

After four years without a winning record, the Ravens broke through in 2000. Led by the league's top-ranked defense, the team won 12 games during the regular season and swept through the AFC play-offs, allowing an average of fewer than 6 points per game in the postseason. The Ravens easily defeated the New York Giants in Super Bowl XXXV the following January, and Lewis was named Most Valuable Player of the game. In addition to Lewis, the Super Bowl–winning Ravens squad featured standouts such as offensive lineman Jonathan Ogden, tight end Shannon Sharpe, and cornerback Rod Woodson. Over the remainder of the decade, the Ravens remained competitive, qualifying for the play-offs in five of the nine seasons after 2000 and featuring a defense ranked in the top five for total yardage allowed in six of those years.

CINCINNATI BENGALS

Based in Cincinnati, Ohio, the Bengals have appeared in two Super Bowls (1982, 1989).

The Bengals joined the AFL as an expansion team in 1968. Paul Brown, who had become one of the most respected coaches in the game at the helm of the Cleveland Browns, was one of the franchise's founders and its first head coach. Cincinnati was a member of the AFL for just two seasons before the league merged with the NFL in 1970.

The Bengals' maiden year in the NFL saw the team post its first winning record and earn a play-off spot as the AFC Central champion. That same year, the team began to play in Riverfront Stadium, a multipurpose venue they would share with baseball's Cincinnati Reds for the following 30 years. In 1972 the Bengals turned their offense over to second-year quarterback Ken Anderson (from tiny Augustana College in Rock Island, Ill.), who would go on to lead the team for over a decade and set numerous franchise passing records. The Bengals made two more play-off appearances in the 1970s, but they failed to win their first contest on each occasion.

Brown resigned as head coach after the 1975 season, but he stayed on as team president until his death in 1991. One of Brown's most important personnel moves came in 1980, when he drafted tackle Anthony Muñoz, who is considered one of the greatest offensive linemen in football history; Muñoz anchored the Bengals' line for 13 seasons. In 1981 the Bengals won a conference-best 12 regular-season games and had their first two postseason wins to advance to Super Bowl XVI the following January, where they lost to the San Francisco 49ers. Cincinnati returned to the play-offs after the strike-shortened 1982 season but lost in their opening-round postseason game.

In 1984 Sam Wyche became the Bengals' head coach, and a year later Anderson ceded Cincinnati's starting quarterback role to Boomer Esiason. In 1988 an Esiason-led Bengals team tied the Buffalo Bills for the best record in the AFC by going 12–4. After defeating the Bills in the AFC championship game, the Bengals squared off against the 49ers in the Super Bowl for a second time and were again denied a championship; San Francisco quarterback Joe Montana led his team to a last-minute 20–16 victory.

Throughout the 1990s the Bengals were widely regarded as one of the worst franchises in the four major North American professional sports leagues. They lost more games than any other NFL team during that decade and were plagued by a series of poor draft choices. The team did not have a winning record for 14 consecutive seasons beginning in 1991 (Wyche's last year as coach). A high

point of this period was the play of Pro Bowl running back
Corey Dillon, but his presence was not enough to prevent
the Bengals from losing at least 10 games in each season
between 1998 and 2002. In 2000 the Bengals moved into a
football-only venue, Paul Brown Stadium.

Cincinnati broke out of its 14-year postseason
drought in 2005, as a team featuring quarterback Carson
Palmer and wide receiver Chad Johnson (known as Chad
Ochocinco from 2008) won a divisional title before losing to the eventual champion Pittsburgh Steelers in the
play-offs. The Bengals captured another division championship in 2009 but again lost their first game of the
postseason—extending the NFL's longest active streak
without a play-off victory, which began in 1991.

Cleveland Browns

Based in Cleveland, the Browns have won four NFL
championships (1950, 1954–55, 1964) and four All-America
Football Conference (AAFC) championships (1946–49).

The Browns were founded in 1946 and, as the result of
a fan contest to choose their moniker, were named after
their first head coach, Paul Brown, who was already a popular figure in Ohio, having coached Ohio State University
to a national collegiate football championship. The
Browns were originally members of the AAFC and won
the league title in each of the four years of the AAFC's
existence. The most notable of these title-winning teams
was the 1948 squad, which went 15–0 to become the first
undefeated team in organized professional football history. The Browns were integrated into the NFL along with
two other former AAFC teams in 1950, and—despite the
prevailing expectations—they continued to have success
in the new league. The Browns' first game in the NFL was
a symbolic 35–10 victory over the defending champion

JIM BROWN

(b. Feb. 17, 1936, St. Simons, Ga., U.S.)

The outstanding professional football running back Jim Brown led the NFL in rushing for eight of his nine seasons in the league. He was the dominant player of his era and one of the small number of running backs rated as the best of all time.

In high school and at Syracuse University in New York, James Nathaniel Brown displayed exceptional all-around athletic ability, excelling in basketball, baseball, track, and lacrosse as well as football. In his final year at Syracuse, Brown earned All-America honours in both football and lacrosse. Many considered Brown's best sport to be lacrosse, and he was inducted into both the Pro Football Hall of Fame and the U.S. Lacrosse National Hall of Fame.

From 1957 through 1965, Brown played for the Cleveland Browns of the NFL, and he led the league in rushing yardage every year except 1962. Standing 6.2 feet (1.88 metres) and weighing 232 pounds (105 kg), Brown was a bruising runner who possessed the speed to outrun opponents as well as the strength to run over them. He rushed for more than 1,000 yards in seven seasons and established NFL single-season records by rushing for 1,527 yards in 1958 (12-game schedule) and 1,863 yards in 1963 (14-game schedule), a record broken by O.J. Simpson in 1973. On Nov. 24, 1957, he set an NFL record by rushing for 237 yards in a single game, and he equaled that total on Nov. 19, 1961. At the close of his career, he had scored 126 touchdowns, 106 by rushing, had gained a record 12,312 yards in 2,359 rushing attempts for an average of 5.22 yards, and had a record combined yardage (rushing along with pass receptions) of 14,811 yards. Brown's rushing and combined yardage records stood until 1984, when both were surpassed by Walter Payton of the Chicago Bears.

At 30 years of age and seemingly at the height of his athletic abilities, Brown retired from football to pursue a career in motion pictures. He appeared in many action and adventure films, among them *The Dirty Dozen* (1967) and *100 Rifles* (1969). Brown was also active in issues facing African Americans, forming groups to assist black-owned businesses and to rehabilitate gang members.

Philadelphia Eagles. The early years of Browns football were defined by the stellar play of quarterback Otto Graham and the innovative coaching of Brown, both members of the Hall of Fame, who guided the team to 10 divisional titles in its first 10 years and seven championships between the two leagues. These early Browns teams also featured Lou "The Toe" Groza, a kicker and offensive lineman, and Marion Motley, a bruising running back who was one of the first African Americans to play professional football.

In 1957 Cleveland drafted Syracuse University running back Jim Brown, who would set every major NFL rushing record during his nine-year career and gain the status of possibly the greatest football player of all time. Cleveland's plans to pair Brown in the backfield with another remarkable running back from Syracuse, Ernie Davis, winner of the 1961 Heisman Trophy, came to naught when Davis contracted leukemia and never played a game for the Browns. Nevertheless, Brown helped the team reach four league championship games, one of which they won (1964). Cleveland advanced to the NFL conference championship game twice in the five seasons after he retired in 1966, but the Browns entered into their first prolonged period of mediocrity in the 1970s, from which they emerged briefly in the 1980 season due to the frequent last-minute heroics of a team dubbed the Kardiac Kids.

Quarterback and Ohio native Bernie Kosar was drafted in 1985 and led the Browns to five appearances in the playoffs in his first five years in the league. The Browns lost two memorable AFC championship games to John Elway and the Denver Broncos during this span, each of which is remembered by Browns fans by an epithet describing the last-minute events responsible for Cleveland's downfall: "The Drive" (1987) and "The Fumble" (1988). The mid-1980s also saw the advent of the Dawg Pound, a section of

Cleveland's Dawg Pound is a section of the stadium reserved for some of the most vocal and ardent Browns fans. Tom Hauck/Getty Images

the end-zone bleachers of the team's home stadium where a rowdy group of often-costumed fans sat, solidifying the image of Browns supporters as some of the most vocal and devoted fans in the NFL.

The 1990s brought much darker times for the Browns. Owner Art Modell—who had been losing money for years because of an unfavourable stadium lease with the city—orchestrated a move that sent the team to Baltimore in 1996, breaking the hearts of Cleveland's many loyal fans and shocking many football observers nationwide. The NFL arranged to keep the Browns' name, logo, colours, and history in Cleveland, and the league promised the city a new team in the near future. Cleveland was without a franchise until 1999, when local businessman Al Lerner purchased an expansion team that assumed the Browns' name, uniforms, and history. While the expansion Browns earned a play-off appearance in 2002, the team has yet to match the success of its previous incarnation.

PITTSBURGH STEELERS

Based in Pittsburgh, the Steelers have won six Super Bowl titles and seven AFC championships. One of the NFL's most successful and storied franchises, the Steelers have more Super Bowl victories than any other team.

Originally called the Pittsburgh Pirates, the team was founded in 1933 by Pittsburgh resident Art Rooney, who allegedly used winnings from a wager on a horse race to establish the franchise. (Ownership of the team remains within the Rooney family to this day.) The team was not an early success; it qualified for the play-offs just once in its first 37 years. In 1940 the team changed its nickname to "Steelers" in tribute to Pittsburgh's main industry. The Steelers tied for the NFL Eastern Division title in 1947, but they were shut out 21–0 by the Philadelphia Eagles in a play-off match to qualify for the NFL championship game. Rooney watched the Steelers struggle through the 1950s and '60s until their fortunes turned around with the arrival of head coach Chuck Noll in 1969.

From 1969 to 1972 Noll showcased his amazing skill at recognizing talent as he drafted five future Hall of Famers: defensive tackle "Mean" Joe Greene, quarterback Terry Bradshaw, defensive back Mel Blount, linebacker Jack Ham, and running back Franco Harris (remembered for his "Immaculate Reception," a game-winning catch in the play-offs against the Oakland Raiders in 1972, one of the most remarkable and controversial plays in professional football history). In 1974 Noll selected four more players who would eventually be inducted into the Hall of Fame: centre Mike Webster, receivers Lynn Swann and John Stallworth, and linebacker Jack Lambert. These players went on to form a dynasty of unmatched success, winning four Super Bowls (1975, 1976, 1979, and 1980) in six seasons behind a dominant defense known as the "Steel Curtain" and an efficient offense led by Bradshaw. The Steelers teams of the 1970s were also characterized by a fervent fan base, notable for the bright yellow "Terrible Towels"—which were created by the team's popular and idiosyncratic radio broadcaster for 35 years, Myron Cope—that fans would wave during home games. Pittsburgh faded slightly in the 1980s, with four post season berths in the decade, and Noll retired in 1991.

Noll was replaced by Bill Cowher, who led the Steelers to the play-offs in 10 of his 15 seasons with the team. One of Cowher's most significant personnel moves was his promotion of secondary coach Dick LeBeau to the position of defensive coordinator in 1995: in his two stints (1995–97, 2004–) as the Steelers' coordinator,

JOE GREENE

(b. Sept. 24, 1946, Temple, Texas, U.S.)

Joe Greene who is widely considered one of the greatest defensive linemen in NFL history.

Charles Edward Greene was a consensus All-American defensive tackle at North Texas State University (now known as the University of North Texas) in 1968, and he was chosen by the Pittsburgh Steelers with the fourth overall selection of the 1969 NFL draft. Once he joined the Steelers after a contract holdout, Greene was an instant success on the field—he was named Defensive Rookie of the Year for 1969—but his frequent temperamental outbursts led to charges of immaturity. While Greene continued to play with an aggressive streak throughout his career (leading to his famous "Mean Joe Greene" nickname), his ever-increasing dominance of opposing offensive linemen—buttressed by his thoughtful and gracious off-field demeanour—served to stem doubts about his ability to thrive in the NFL.

Throughout the 1970s Greene served as the anchor of Pittsburgh's famed "Steel Curtain" defense and was a key player in four Steelers Super Bowl victories (1975, 1976, 1979, 1980). Over the course of his 13-year career, all of which was with the Steelers, he was voted to 10 Pro Bowls and was twice named the NFL's Defensive Player of the Year (1972, 1974). After his retirement in 1982, Greene spent time as an assistant coach for a number of NFL teams, and the Steelers hired him as a special assistant to their scouting department in 2004.

Greene also acted in several television programs and films both during and after his playing days. He was especially noted for a 1979 television commercial for Coca-Cola that featured a battered post-game Greene being offered a bottle of the soft drink by a young fan who is in turn rewarded—in an oft-replayed and parodied moment—by Greene's tossing him his jersey. In 1987 Greene was inducted into the Pro Football Hall of Fame.

LeBeau put together formidable defenses that defined the Pittsburgh teams of those eras. The Steelers' defense of the mid-1990s was highlighted by stars such as future Hall of Fame cornerback Rod Woodson and linebackers

Greg Lloyd and Kevin Greene. Pittsburgh advanced to the Super Bowl in 1996 but lost to the Dallas Cowboys. The Steelers continued their success into the new century, and in 2006—with a team featuring quarterback Ben Roethlisberger, wide receiver Hines Ward, and safety Troy Polamalu—they defeated the Seattle Seahawks to gain a fifth Super Bowl title. In 2009 the Steelers, under the leadership of second-year head coach Mike Tomlin, beat the Arizona Cardinals in dramatic fashion to capture their record sixth Super Bowl championship.

After missing the play-offs following the 2009 regular season, Pittsburgh captured its third AFC championship in a six-year span in 2011 to earn a berth in Super Bowl XLV against the Green Bay Packers. There, the Steelers lost a Super Bowl for just the second time in team history, as Green Bay prevailed 31–26.

AFC South

Houston Texans

Based in Houston, the Texans are the youngest franchise in the NFL.

Houston-area businessmen began their efforts to create the franchise that would become the Texans in 1997, when the NFL's Houston Oilers relocated to Tennessee. The NFL awarded an expansion franchise to Houston in 1999. The team's first game came in 2002, with a victory over the established cross-state power (and presumed rival) Dallas Cowboys. That win was one of just four in the team's inaugural season, and the Texans finished their first year in the league at the bottom of the divisional standings. The 2002 campaign was the beginning of a trend, as the team placed last (or tied for last) in the AFC South in five of its first six seasons of existence and became arguably best known for possessing a porous offensive line that in 2002 allowed a record number of sacks of quarterback David Carr—who repeated as the league's most-sacked quarterback in 2004 and 2005.

In 2009, behind a powerful offensive line led by dominant wide receiver Andre Johnson and standout quarterback Matt Schaub, the Texans posted the first winning record (9–7) in franchise history.

INDIANAPOLIS COLTS

Currently based in Indianapolis, but originally located in Baltimore, Md., the Colts have won three NFL championships (1958, 1959, 1968) and two Super Bowls (1971, 2007).

The Colts originated from the dissolved Dallas Texans NFL team in 1953. There had been two professional football teams with the name Baltimore Colts before 1953, and continued fan support in the Baltimore area led the NFL to approve the purchase and relocation of the defunct Texans by the Baltimore-based owners. The rechristened Colts hired future Hall of Fame head coach Weeb Ewbank in 1954 and signed Johnny Unitas, who became one of football's all-time greatest quarterbacks, in 1956.

In the late 1950s Unitas headed a formidable offense that featured, in addition to Unitas, three other future Hall of Famers: tackle Jim Parker, end Raymond Berry, and halfback Lenny Moore. In 1958 the Colts defeated the New York Giants 23–17 in a nationally televised NFL championship game, which the Colts won when their running back Alan Ameche scored a one-yard touchdown run in a sudden-death overtime period. The 1958 championship game took on the nickname "The Greatest Game Ever Played" and was likely the single most important moment in the popularization of professional football in the latter half of the 20th century. The Colts reemerged as

NFL champions the following season, beating the Giants again in the championship game.

The team appeared in another memorable title game in 1969, when the heavily favoured NFL champion Colts met the upstart AFL champion New York Jets in Super Bowl III. The Jets were led by young quarterback Joe Namath, who said, before the game, that he guaranteed a Super Bowl victory and then guided his 18-point underdog team to the biggest upset in Super Bowl history. In 1971 the Colts won their first Super Bowl, a 16–13 victory over the Dallas Cowboys.

The years after Unitas's 1973 departure from the team were filled with many mediocre seasons and no play-off victories for the remainder of the team's tenure in Baltimore. In 1984 team owner Robert Irsay—after failing to get local government funding for a new stadium—relocated the team to Indianapolis in a move that took place in the middle of the night, before most Colt fans knew that any move had been planned. Even after the franchise had departed, the Colts Marching Band kept the spirit of the team alive in Baltimore by continuing to perform in parades and at civic events until 1996, when the Cleveland Browns moved to the city as the Ravens.

The relocated Colts initially struggled, qualifying for postseason play only once in their first 11 seasons in Indianapolis. In 1998 the Colts drafted quarterback Peyton Manning, who teamed with wide receiver Marvin Harrison and running back Edgerrin James to give the Colts one of the league's best offenses in the early 2000s. Manning put up record passing numbers and led the team to numerous winning seasons, but he was often blamed for his team's failures to advance in the play-offs.

The team broke through in 2007, beating the Chicago Bears in the Super Bowl and putting a stop to criticism that Manning could not win the big game.

JOHNNY UNITAS

Johnny Unitas. Walter Iooss Jr./Sports Illustrated/Getty Images

(b. May 7, 1933, Pittsburgh, Pa., U.S.—d. Sept. 11, 2002, Timonium, Md.)

Johnny Unitas is considered to be one of the greatest all-time NFL quarterbacks.

John Constantine Unitas excelled in football at St. Justin's High School in Pittsburgh, but his slight stature (he weighed only 145 pounds [66 kg]) prevented him from earning an athletic scholarship to the University of Notre Dame. He instead played for the University of Louisville (Ky.), where he grew to 6 feet 1 inch (1.85 metres) and 190 pounds (86 kg). Unitas became Louisville's starting quarterback during his freshman season, but he played on mediocre teams throughout his collegiate career and was not considered a great pro prospect upon his graduation. He was selected by the NFL's Pittsburgh Steelers in the ninth round of the 1955 draft but was released before the regular season began. He worked at construction jobs and played for a semiprofessional team in the Pittsburgh area for $6 a game until he was signed by the Baltimore Colts in 1956.

Unitas was thrust into the starting role after the Colt's quarterback broke his leg during the fourth game of Unitas's rookie season. In his second year he led the NFL in passing yards and touchdowns and was selected for the first of 10 career Pro Bowls. Unitas's rise to stardom from such lowly beginnings made him the quintessential rags-to-riches hero as professional football emerged as the top spectator sport in the United States in the 1960s. His legendary status was cemented by his performance in the 1958 championship game, in which he led the Colts to a 23–17 overtime victory over the New York Giants. The dramatic game, viewed by a national television audience, is regarded as a key step in the NFL's rise in popularity. Unitas and the Colts also took part in what is arguably the other most significant game in the ascent of the NFL: an upset loss to the AFL's New York Jets in the 1969 Super Bowl.

Unitas, whose black high-top shoes and distinctive backpedal became his signature, led the Colts to three NFL championships (1958, 1959, 1968) and one Super Bowl victory (1971). He led the league four times each in passing yards and in touchdown passes and retired with career NFL records for passing yards, touchdowns, and completions (all of which have since been broken). Unitas was traded to the San Diego Chargers in 1973, his last season. "Johnny U" was elected to the Pro Football Hall of Fame in 1979.

In 2009 the Colts won their first 14 games of the season en route to earning the AFC's top seed in the play-offs. Indianapolis then easily advanced to the Super Bowl, where they were upset by the New Orleans Saints. The Colts were in the play-off hunt again after the 2010 regular season, but lost in the first round due to a last-second field goal by the New York Jets, 17–16.

JACKSONVILLE JAGUARS

Based in Jacksonville, Fla., the Jaguars appeared in the AFC championship game in just their second year of existence.

The Jaguars began play in 1995 as an expansion team alongside the Carolina Panthers of the NFC. The Jaguars' first college draft pick was future All-Pro tackle Tony Boselli, who would serve as the anchor of a productive offense that helped the Jaguars quickly become a winning franchise. After posting a 4–12 record in their inaugural season, the Jaguars went 9–7 and earned a spot in the AFC play-offs the following season behind the standout play of quarterback Mark Brunell and wide receiver Jimmy Smith. The team then proceeded to win two postseason games on the road before losing to the New England Patriots in the AFC championship game. After again qualifying for the play-offs in 1997, the Jaguars added running back Fred Taylor to their dynamic offense in 1998 and won their first division title that season. The following year the team's 14–2 record was the best in the NFL, but Jacksonville was upset by their division rival Tennessee Titans in the AFC championship game.

The phenomenal start of the Jaguars franchise slowed in the early 2000s, as the team won no more than seven games in any season between 2000 and 2003. In 2005 and 2007 the Jaguars returned to the postseason but were eliminated by the Patriots on each occasion.

TENNESSEE TITANS

Based in Nashville, the Titans have appeared in one Super Bowl (2000). The franchise was located in Houston and was known as the Oilers from 1960 to 1996, during which time it won two AFL championships (1960, 1961).

The Oilers were one of the eight original AFL teams when the upstart league was founded in 1960. Led by quarterback George Blanda, they won the inaugural AFL title and repeated as champions the following year. The team returned to a third consecutive AFL title game in 1962, but they lost a close contest in double overtime to the Dallas Texans. The Oilers then posted four consecutive losing seasons, and Blanda was released in 1967 after the team won only 3 of their 14 games in 1966. Houston rebounded to make play-off appearances in 1967 and 1969.

The 1970s brought an AFL-NFL merger and a downturn in the Oilers' fortunes, as the team won just one game in 1972 and again in 1973. Houston slowly improved over the course of the decade, and, after colourful head coach Bum Phillips was hired in 1975 to reinvigorate the team, they returned to the postseason in 1978. Behind an offense featuring bruising running back Earl Campbell and flashy wide receiver and kick returner Billy "White Shoes" Johnson and a defense led by linebacker Robert Brazile and end Elvin Bethea, the Oilers teams of the late 1970s enraptured the Houston fan base. These "Luv Ya Blue" Oilers (nicknamed for the fans' adoration of the blue-clad team) advanced to conference championship games after the 1978 and 1979 seasons but were defeated on each occasion by the Pittsburgh Steelers. A less-successful play-off berth came in 1980, and the Oilers quickly fell back toward the bottom of the AFC standings during the early to mid-1980s.

The Oilers signed quarterback Warren Moon out of the Canadian Football League in 1984, and the team soon boasted one of the most high-powered offenses in the league, also anchored by Hall of Fame lineman Bruce Matthews. Moon led the Oilers to seven straight postseason berths from 1987 to 1993, but they did not manage to advance to a single conference championship in that span. The frustrated Oilers ownership then traded away many of the team's best players, including Moon, and the team posted a 2–14 win-loss record during the 1994 season. During that year the Oilers promoted to head coach defensive coordinator Jeff Fisher, who would go on to have the longest coaching tenure in team history and oversee the franchise's most successful period.

Fisher's first seasons in charge were overshadowed by the team ownership's desire to have the city of Houston build a new football-only stadium and the Oilers' subsequent relocation to Nashville in 1997. The Oilers played

EARL CAMPBELL

(b. March 29, 1955, Tyler, Texas, U.S.)

Running back Earl Campbell is known for his bruising running style, which made him one of the most dominant rushers in the history of the sport despite his relatively short career.

Campbell was raised in poverty alongside 10 siblings in rural Texas. He was a hotly recruited high school football player and ended up at the University of Texas (Austin). He was a four-year starter in college, earning all-conference honours in each season and consensus All-American honours in 1977, and he won the Heisman Trophy as the best player in college football after his senior season. The Houston Oilers traded for the first overall selection in the 1978 NFL draft, which they used to pick Campbell, who was already popular with much of the team's fan base following his collegiate exploits in nearby Austin.

Weighing 230 pounds (104 kg) and having massive 36-inch (91-cm) thighs, Campbell was a punishing runner who often needed to be tackled by multiple defenders to be brought down. He was named the NFL's Offensive Rookie of the Year after rushing for a league-high 1,450 yards and helping the Oilers reach the conference championship game in his first season with the team. Campbell led the NFL in rushing yards and rushing touchdowns in 1979 and 1980, and he was named the league's Most Valuable Player in 1979. He was voted first-team All-Pro in each of his first three seasons and was named to the Pro Bowl in five of his first six seasons. Campbell's high number of carries (his 373 in 1980 was an NFL record at the time), however, took their toll, and his play began to fall off soon before his midseason trade to the New Orleans Saints in 1984. He retired from professional football following the 1985 season.

Campbell's career lasted just eight seasons. The serious health issues he experienced, due to the years of abuse he subjected his body to on the gridiron, were well publicized after his retirement. He was afflicted by a number of chronic conditions, including severe arthritis and a bad back, and was forced to use a cane to walk beginning in his late 40s. He was nevertheless able to run a successful meat products company and serve as a special assistant to the athletic director at the University of Texas in the years after he left the NFL. Campbell was inducted into the Pro Football Hall of Fame in 1991.

one season in Memphis and one in Nashville at Vanderbilt University's football stadium before their home stadium was completed prior to the 1999 season. The team was then rechristened the Tennessee Titans, a name derived from Nashville's sobriquet of "the Athens of the South."

The Titans won 13 games in 1999 behind the standout play of quarterback Steve McNair and running back Eddie George, and the team's first play-off game in Nashville ended in memorable fashion. Trailing the Buffalo Bills by a point with 16 seconds remaining, the Titans fielded a short kickoff, and tight end Frank Wycheck threw a lateral across the field to receiver Kevin Dyson, who easily scored a game-winning 75-yard touchdown in a play that became known as the "Music City Miracle." The Titans then won two additional road play-off games to earn the franchise's first Super Bowl berth. In the Super Bowl the Titans again found themselves trailing their opponent (the St. Louis Rams) with seconds remaining, and the game ended with Dyson being dramatically tackled at the 1-yard line as he attempted to score the tying touchdown. The Titans returned to the postseason in three of the next four seasons and advanced to the AFC championship game in 2002 (a loss to the Oakland Raiders).

After a few losing seasons, in 2007 the Titans again established themselves as one of the AFC's best teams. In 2008 they won 13 games to post the best record in the NFL but were upset at home by the Baltimore Ravens in the first round of the play-offs.

AFC West

Denver Broncos

Based in Denver, the Broncos have won six AFC championships and two Super Bowls (1998, 1999).

The Broncos were founded in 1960 as one of the original members of the AFL. During the league's 10 years of existence, the Broncos never posted a winning record, and they finished last in their division on six occasions. The team did have a few standout players at this time, however, including wide receiver Lionel Taylor, who led the AFL in receptions five times, and running back Floyd Little. After the 1970 AFL-NFL merger, the Broncos continued to dwell in the divisional cellar before having their first winning season in 1973.

The Broncos finally broke through to gain a play-off berth in 1977. Led by linebackers Randy Gradishar and Tom Jackson, as well as the rest of the so-called "Orange Crush" defense—whose name derived from the team's bright orange home jerseys at the time—the Broncos went 12–2 and claimed the best record in the conference. They won their first two postseason games to advance to the Super Bowl, which they lost to the Dallas Cowboys. Denver returned to the play-offs the following two seasons but lost their first game on both occasions. The team's sudden ascent to the upper echelon of the AFC led to heightened expectations, and, after the Broncos finished 8–8 in 1980 after their three-game postseason streak, head coach Red Miller was fired and replaced by Dan Reeves. In 1983 Reeves oversaw the trade for disgruntled Baltimore Colts draftee John Elway, who would go on to star as the Broncos' quarterback for 16 seasons and become the most iconic player in franchise history.

With Elway leading the offense and Pro Bowl linebacker Karl Mecklenburg anchoring the defense, the Broncos became one of the most successful NFL teams of the 1980s. Denver advanced to three Super Bowls in the decade, and their consecutive AFC championship games against the Cleveland Browns in 1987 and 1988 were two of the most memorable contests of the time. The former

The arrival of Dan Reeves (left, front) *and quarterback John Elway during the 1980s boosted the Denver Broncos into the upper echelon of the NFL.* George Rose/Getty Images

game featured Elway leading the Broncos 98 yards in the fourth quarter to tie the score and eventually win in overtime (which became known as "The Drive"), and the latter was decided when Browns running back Earnest Byner lost the ball on Denver's 3-yard line with just over a minute remaining as he attempted to score a tying touchdown ("The Fumble"). However, the Broncos were not able to capitalize on these thrilling championship game victories and were soundly beaten (by the New York Giants and the Washington Redskins, respectively) in each season's subsequent Super Bowl. The Broncos returned to the Super Bowl in 1990, but they were defeated by the San Francisco 49ers by a score of 55–10, the worst loss in Super Bowl history. Reeves's failure to win a Super Bowl—compounded by his years of feuding with Elway—led to his dismissal after the 1992 season.

Denver's former offensive coordinator Mike Shanahan was hired as the team's head coach in 1995. With a talented roster including running back Terrell Davis, wide receiver Rod Smith, and tight end Shannon Sharpe, the Broncos were one of the premier offenses in the NFL during Shanahan's first seasons with the team, and in 1998 they again were the AFC's representative in the Super Bowl. This time the well-balanced Broncos squad upset the Green Bay Packers to capture the franchise's first title. Denver won a team-record 14 games the next season, which it followed with a second Super Bowl victory (over the Atlanta Falcons). Elway then retired, and Denver finished last in their division the following season. The team went to the postseason in four of the six years between 2000 and 2005 but advanced past the first round only once and lost in the AFC championship that season (2005). After three consecutive years of missing the playoffs, Shanahan was fired after the 2008 season, and the Broncos began a thorough rebuilding effort.

KANSAS CITY CHIEFS

Based in Kansas City, Mo., the Chiefs won three AFL championships (1962, 1966, 1969) and Super Bowl IV.

The team, originally based in Dallas and known as the Texans, was one of eight founding franchises when the AFL came into existence in 1960. The Texans were owned by Lamar Hunt, who—after having been rebuked in his earlier attempt to purchase the NFL's Chicago Cardinals—initiated the founding of the AFL by organizing other prospective NFL owners who had been turned down by the established league. Hunt hired Hank Stram to serve as the Texans' first head coach, and Stram led the team to two middle-of-the-road finishes in its first two seasons. The Texans brought in quarterback Len Dawson (like Stram a future Hall of Famer) before the 1962 season, and Dallas went 11–3 that year, defeating the Houston Oilers in the AFL championship game. Despite the team's success, the Dallas market was not able to sustain two football franchises (the other being the NFL's Dallas Cowboys), and Hunt decided to relocate the Texans to Kansas City in 1963.

The newly renamed Chiefs returned to the middle of the AFL West standings until 1966. That season they again won 11 games and captured the AFL title. The Chiefs were then a part of one of the most historic moments in football history when they faced off against the Green Bay Packers in the first annual AFL-NFL World Championship Game (which would later be renamed the "Super Bowl" by Hunt), which they lost 35–10. In 1969 the Chiefs featured the league's leading defense—which starred future Hall of Famers Willie Lanier, Bobby Bell, and Buck Buchanan—and they once again won an AFL championship and earned a berth into the Super Bowl. At the Super Bowl the Chiefs defeated the Minnesota Vikings in what

WILLIE LANIER

(b. Aug. 21, 1945, Clover, Va., U.S.)

An outstanding defensive player for the Kansas City Chiefs in the 1960s and '70s, Willie Lanier overturned the stereotype that African Americans could not handle the key defensive position of middle linebacker.

Lanier was named to the Little All-America team (for players in small-college programs) while at Morgan State University (Baltimore, Md.). In 1967 the Chiefs selected him in the second round of the first combined AFL and NFL draft. The Chiefs had lost 35–10 to the Green Bay Packers in the first Super Bowl earlier that year and focused on defensive players in the draft.

Lanier became the starting middle linebacker in his rookie season, which was cut short by an injury. The next year, the Chiefs were 12–2, and Lanier began a streak of eight consecutive Pro Bowl selections. In his third season, Lanier led the Chiefs to the final AFL championship prior to the league's merging with the NFL. As AFL champions, the Chiefs unexpectedly defeated the Minnesota Vikings in Super Bowl IV in 1970, with Lanier making an interception and the defense shutting out Minnesota in the first half on the way to a 23–7 victory.

While the Chiefs made the play-offs just one more time in his career, Lanier remained a defensive star in the league. Called "Honey Bear" by his teammates, Lanier was a ferocious tackler. After concussions early in his career, he wore a specially padded helmet to protect himself from his own tremendous collisions. He had 15 career fumble recoveries and 27 pass interceptions, with 2 returned for touchdowns. Lanier was enshrined in the Pro Football Hall of Fame in 1986.

was the final game ever played by an AFL franchise, as the two leagues merged in 1970. Kansas City made another play-off appearance in 1971 but then entered a period that saw the team post losing records in nine of the 14 seasons between 1972 and 1985 and miss the postseason in each of those years.

In 1989 the Chiefs hired head coach Marty Schottenheimer and drafted linebacker Derrick Thomas.

Schottenheimer guided Kansas City to a play-off berth in his second season with the team, and in 1993, led by quarterback Joe Montana, the Chiefs advanced to the AFC championship game, which they lost to the Buffalo Bills. With Thomas and defensive end Neil Smith anchoring a stout defense, the Chiefs won an NFL-best 13 games in 1995, but they were upset in their opening play-off contest by the Indianapolis Colts. The Chiefs tied for the best record in the league in 1997 but were again defeated in their first play-off game, this time by the division rival Denver Broncos. After a five-year postseason drought, Kansas City—with a high-scoring offense featuring running back Priest Holmes and tight end Tony Gonzalez—again won 13 games and a division crown in 2003. Once again a stellar regular season was followed by play-off disappointment as the Chiefs were once again upset at home by the Colts. The team then had a series of moderately successful years, including another postseason berth (and first-round loss) in 2006, before an abrupt slide resulted in a franchise-worst 2–14 record in 2008 and the hiring of a new front office and coaching staff.

Oakland Raiders

Based in Oakland, Calif., the Raiders have won three Super Bowl championships (1977, 1981, 1984), one AFL championship (1967), and four AFC titles. Viewed by many as the "villains" of the NFL because of their historic tendency for rough play, the Raiders embody the motto coined by longtime owner Al Davis: "Just win, baby."

The Raiders were founded in 1960 as one of the eight original teams of the AFL. After three losing seasons, the franchise hired Davis in 1963 to serve as the team's head coach and general manager. He implemented a "vertical" passing attack, which relied on long throws downfield to stretch the opposing defense, and quickly turned the team into a contender. After a three-month stint as AFL commissioner in 1966, Davis became a part-owner of the Raiders, and he began buying out (and, in some cases, forcing out) the other owners, ultimately gaining complete control of the team in 1976.

With an offense starring quarterback Daryle Lamonica and centre Jim Otto, the Raiders won the AFL championship in December 1967, a victory that sent the team to its first Super Bowl the following January (a loss to the Green Bay Packers). John Madden was hired as head coach in 1969, and under his guidance the Raiders became an elite team, posting consecutive winning seasons during Madden's 10-year tenure with the team and taking the franchise's first Super Bowl (1977). It was during this period that the Raiders forged an image as a team of tough, take-no-prisoners players—such as future Hall of Fame offensive linemen Jim Otto, Gene Upshaw, and Art Shell; linebacker Ted "The Stork" Hendricks; defensive end Ben Davidson; and cornerback Willie Brown—who would occasionally cross the line into dirty play. Those teams also featured an additional trio of future Hall of Fame players in tight end Dave Casper, kicker George Blanda, and wide receiver Fred Biletnikoff, as well as fiery quarterback Ken "The Snake" Stabler. Madden's successor, Tom Flores (who was the Raiders' first starting quarterback), shepherded the team to another Super Bowl victory in 1981.

Davis had been long upset about the conditions of the Raiders' home stadium when, in 1980, he signed a memorandum of agreement promising to move the franchise to Los Angeles. The NFL blocked the move, but Davis won a landmark antitrust lawsuit against the league in 1982, and the Raiders immediately relocated. The team qualified for the play-offs in each of their first four seasons in Los Angeles, which included another Super Bowl title in 1984. The teams of the 1980s featured three future Hall

GENE UPSHAW

(b. Aug. 15, 1945, Robstown, Texas, U.S.—d. Aug. 20, 2008, near Lake Tahoe, Calif.)

Gene Upshaw was a Hall of Fame offensive lineman for the Oakland Raiders before serving as the executive director of the NFL Players Association (NFLPA; 1983–2008).

Eugene Thurman Upshaw, Jr., played only one year of high school football, but he earned an athletic scholarship to Texas College of Arts and Industries (now Texas A&M University–Kingsville) after an impressive tryout for the football team. Following a successful collegiate career, he was chosen by the Raiders in the first round of the 1967 NFL draft. In Oakland, Upshaw formed a dominant left side of the Raiders' offensive line with tackle (and fellow Hall of Fame member) Art Shell, and he was a member of two Super Bowl-winning squads (1977, 1981) and was a seven-time Pro Bowl selection (1968, 1972–77).

After serving as the Raiders' player representative to the NFLPA, Upshaw was named president of the union in 1980. He retired from the Raiders after the 1981 season, and two years later he became the first African American head of a major players' union when he took over as executive director of the NFLPA. In his new role, Upshaw oversaw a short-lived and ultimately unsuccessful players' strike in 1987, and he figured prominently in the negotiations that brought full free agency—the ability of a player to freely sign with any team when his contract expires—to the NFL in 1993; free agency became a key feature of the league at the turn of the 21st century. In 1994 he helped launch National Football League Players, Inc., an association that greatly increased the marketing and licensing power of NFL players. Upshaw was inducted into the Pro Football Hall of Fame in 1987.

of Famers—running back Marcus Allen, defensive lineman Howie Long, and cornerback Mike Haynes—and multisport sensation Bo Jackson, who excelled in both Major League Baseball and the NFL. Davis soured on the stadium in Los Angeles over the years, and he moved the franchise back to Oakland in 1995. The Raiders struggled in the years after their second move, but, behind a high-powered offense led by quarterback Rich Gannon and wide receivers Tim Brown and Jerry Rice, they advanced to the Super Bowl in 2003, which they lost to the Tampa Bay Buccaneers. Since 2003 the franchise has been marked by a lack of success on the field, poor personnel decisions, and a fractious front office, all of which considerably damaged the famed Raiders' mystique.

SAN DIEGO CHARGERS

Based in San Diego, the Chargers have appeared in one Super Bowl (1995).

Originally based in Los Angeles, the Chargers began play in 1960 as one of the original eight members of the upstart AFL. The Chargers went 10–4 in their first season and advanced to the inaugural AFL championship game, which they lost to the Houston Oilers. After just one year in Los Angeles, the team relocated to San Diego, where their success continued as they won 12 of their 14 games and again appeared in the AFL title game (and again lost to the Oilers).

The key to the Chargers' early good fortunes was head coach Sid Gillman, one of the most innovative minds in the history of football, who led the team from their inaugural year through most of 1969 and for part of the 1971 season; he also served as the Chargers' general manager from 1960 to 1971. Gillman, as coach of the NFL's Los Angeles Rams from 1955 to 1959, had developed the first offense to centre around the downfield pass. He brought this proficient offense to the AFL when he took over the Chargers, and his high-scoring team won division crowns in five of the league's first six seasons.

In 1963 San Diego—featuring future Hall of Famers Lance Alworth at wide receiver and Ron Mix at offensive tackle, along with quarterback John Hadl and running back Paul Lowe—won its only AFL title, defeating the

Boston Patriots 51–10 in the championship game. During the mid-1960s the Chargers' play fell off slightly, and, despite finishing with winning records from 1966 through the end of the decade, they never returned to the AFL championships.

The AFL merged with the NFL in 1970, and the Chargers struggled in the expanded league. They did not have a winning season in their first eight years in the NFL, as the team's formerly potent offense became one of the worst in the league.

The Chargers began to return to past form when they hired Don Coryell as head coach five games into the 1978 season. Coryell reinvigorated the play of quarterback Dan Fouts, who became the centrepiece of an aerial attack that led the league in passing yards for a record six consecutive seasons (1978–83). Also featuring superstars wide receiver Charlie Joiner and tight end Kellen Winslow, the San Diego offense (nicknamed "Air Coryell") propelled the Chargers to four straight postseason berths between 1979 and 1982. San Diego played in two conference championship games over this span, which was highlighted by a defeat of the Miami Dolphins in a seesaw 41–38 divisional play-off contest in January 1982 that many consider one of the greatest NFL games of all time. However, the Coryell Chargers failed to advance to the Super Bowl. Coryell resigned during the 1986 season, amid a nine-year postseason drought for the Chargers.

San Diego's return to the play-offs after the 1992 season was notable, as it was the first time in NFL history that a team started with an 0–4 record and rallied to earn a postseason berth. The Chargers lost to the Dolphins in their second play-off game that year. Their postseason run after the 1994 season was much more successful. Led by a defense starring All-Pro linebacker Junior Seau, San Diego won a divisional title and upset the Pittsburgh Steelers in the AFC championship game en route to the franchise's first Super Bowl berth. There they lost soundly to the San Francisco 49ers, 49–26.

The Chargers soon entered one of the worst stretches in franchise history, losing at least 11 games in four of the five years between 1997 and 2001, including a 1–15 season in 2000. The silver lining of the team's disastrous 2000 season was that the Chargers were in a position to draft running back LaDainian Tomlinson and quarterback Drew Brees in the 2001 NFL draft, and the duo led San Diego back to the play-offs after the 2004 season. Chargers teams featuring Tomlinson, quarterback Philip Rivers, and tight end Antonio Gates have had great regular-season success—including four consecutive AFC West titles from 2006 to 2009—but have failed to advance to the Super Bowl.

SUPER BOWL

The Super Bowl is the championship game of the NFL, played by the winners of the AFC and NFC each January or February. The game is hosted by a different city each year.

The game grew out of the merger of the NFL and rival American Football League (AFL) in 1966. The agreement called for an end-of-season championship game, and, although the merger was not finalized until 1970, the first such game, then called the AFL-NFL World Championship Game, was played at the Los Angeles Memorial Coliseum on Jan. 15, 1967. Broadcast on two television networks and played before less than a sellout crowd, the game saw the NFL's Green Bay Packers defeat the AFL's Kansas City Chiefs, 35–10. The name "Super Bowl" first appeared in 1969, as did the use of Roman numerals, which, because the game is played in a different year from the season it culminates, are used to designate the individual games.

The day of the Super Bowl game, known as Super Bowl Sunday, has evolved into an unofficial American holiday, with viewing parties held in homes, taverns, and restaurants throughout the country. The week prior to the game is highlighted by extensive media buildup and a festival atmosphere in the host city. The game itself is accompanied by elaborate pregame and halftime ceremonies and entertainment.

All Super Bowls since the first have been sellouts and consistent TV-ratings leaders, with many Super Bowls among the highest-rated televised sporting events of all time. As a result, commercial time during the game is the most expensive of the year; for example, in 2005 a 30-second spot cost approximately $2.4 million. The high-profile advertisements have featured celebrities and noted filmmakers as well as new technologies in hopes of making an impression on the huge Super Bowl audience. Since the 1980s, media scrutiny of and public interest in Super Bowl commercials have nearly matched that accorded the game itself.

CHAPTER 5
SELECTED PRO FOOTBALL HALL OF FAMERS, 1963 THROUGH 1990

The Pro Football Hall of Fame opened on Sept. 7, 1963, in Canton, Ohio, the city in which the NFL (then the American Professional Football Association) was founded in 1920. Potential Hall of Famers become eligible five years after they retire from either playing or coaching; owners and other contributors to the sport have no such restriction. The following chapter contains biographies, arranged by induction year, of notable Hall of Famers who joined that institution in its first 28 years of existence.

CAL HUBBARD

(b. Oct. 31, 1900, Keytesville, Mo., U.S.—d. Oct. 17, 1977, St. Petersburg, Fla.)

Cal Hubbard was a collegiate and professional football player and American League (AL) baseball umpire, the only person elected to the collegiate and professional football Halls of Fame (1962, 1963) as well as the Baseball Hall of Fame (1976).

Robert Calvin Hubbard was an admirer of coach Bo McMillin and played football for him at Centenary College (Shreveport, La.) and Geneva College (Beaver Falls, Pa.).

McMillin called Hubbard, who was named All-American at tackle (1926–27), the best football player, collegiate or professional, he had ever seen. From 1927 until 1936, Hubbard played in the NFL with the New York Giants, the Green Bay Packers, and the Pittsburgh Pirates (later the Steelers). He was a key part of four title-winning teams—as an end on a devastating 1927 Giants defense that allowed just 20 points in 13 games, and also as a stalwart left tackle on Packers squads that won three straight NFL championships from 1929 to 1931. He was named to the NFL All-Time team in 1969.

During football off-seasons, Hubbard umpired in baseball minor leagues from 1925 through 1935; in 1936 he moved up to the American League. He retired from the field in 1951 after being struck in the eye by a shotgun pellet in a hunting accident. Thereafter he was supervisor of American League umpires until 1968. He also served on the Official Playing Rules Committee (1959–69).

DON HUTSON

(b. Jan. 31, 1913, Pine Bluff, Ark., U.S.—d. June 26, 1997, Rancho Mirage, Calif.)

In his 11-year career in the NFL, from 1935 to 1945, Don Hutson defined the role of the receiver in the modern passing game and created many of the sport's pass routes. In addition to playing wide receiver, he was a skilled place-kicker and defensive safety.

After graduation from the University of Alabama, Donald Montgomery Hutson played with the Green Bay Packers of the NFL (1935–45). He led the league in scoring for five consecutive years (1940–44), in touchdowns eight times (1935–38, 1941–44), in pass receptions eight times (1936–37, 1939, and 1941–45), and in yards gained by pass receptions seven times (1936, 1938–39, and 1941–44).

Though Hutson was slight of build, his speed, precision routes, and reliable hands tormented opposing defenses; he became the first player in the NFL to be covered by two or more defenders. In 1942, his greatest season, he set NFL records (subsequently tied or broken) by catching 74 passes for 1,211 yards and 17 touchdowns; he also kicked 33 points after touchdown and one field goal for a total of 138 points, which remained the NFL single-season scoring record until 1960. From Sept. 12, 1937, to Dec. 2, 1945, he caught at least one pass in each of 95 consecutive games.

Hutson was chosen a member of the NFL's All-Pro team nine times and was named the league's Most Valuable Player in 1941 and 1942. Upon his retirement he held NFL career records of 823 points, 105 total touchdowns, 99 touchdowns on passes caught, 488 pass receptions, and 7,991 yards gained by receiving passes. These records have all since been broken, but the fact that his touchdown receptions mark stood into the late 1980s—long after the landscape of the NFL had drastically changed to emphasize the forward pass—is a testament to how far ahead of his peers Hutson was. He was elected to the Pro Football Hall of Fame in 1963 as a member of the institution's inaugural class and was named to the NFL's 75th Anniversary All-Time Team in 1994.

CURLY LAMBEAU

(b. April 9, 1898, Green Bay, Wisc., U.S.—d. June 1, 1965, Sturgeon Bay, Wisc.)

The football coach Curly Lambeau had one of the longest and most distinguished careers in the history of the game. A founder of the Green Bay Packers in 1919, he served through 1949 as head coach of the only major team in American professional sports to survive in a small city.

A statue of Curly Lambeau stands in front of Green Bay's Lambeau Field, named in his honour. Scott Boehm/Getty Images

After playing briefly for the University of Notre Dame, Earl Louis Lambeau collaborated with George Calhoun, a Green Bay newspaperman, in organizing a professional football team, called the Packers because it received a subsidy from a local meat-packing firm. In 1921 the Packers entered the American Professional Football Association (which in 1922 became the NFL). Lambeau led the team to six NFL championships (1929–31, 1936, 1939, 1944). In addition to coaching and serving as general manager, he played tailback (1919–29) and was noted as a passer. He then coached the NFL's first strong passing teams, with Arnie Herber throwing to Don Hutson.

Lambeau was dismissed after the 1949 season in a dispute with the Packers' management. He subsequently coached the Chicago Cardinals (1950–51) and the Washington Redskins (1952–53). He was enshrined in the Pro Football Hall of Fame in 1963 with a career record of 229 wins, 134 losses, and 22 ties, the NFL's fourth highest win total at the turn of the 21st century. After his death in 1965, the Green Bay Packers rechristened their stadium Lambeau Field.

ERNIE NEVERS

(b. June 11, 1903, Willow River, Minn., U.S.—d. May 3, 1976, San Rafael, Calif.)

Ernie Nevers was a collegiate and professional football and baseball player and is considered one of the greatest football players of all time.

Ernest Alonzo Nevers played at tackle for Superior (Wis.) High School, and as a fullback at Stanford University (Calif.) he was called by Pop Warner the greatest player he had ever coached. He was All-America (1925) and won 11 letters at Stanford, in baseball and basketball as well as in football. He played professional football with the NFL Duluth Eskimos (1926–28) and with the NFL Chicago Cardinals as a player-coach (1929–31), after which he retired. During his brief career, he was a brilliant iron-man player. His 40 points (six touchdowns, four conversions) scored in a game against the Chicago Bears in 1929 remained a league record into the 21st century. Nevers also played professional baseball as a pitcher with the American League St. Louis Browns (1926–28). After retirement from football as a player, he was coach at Lafayette College (Easton, Pa.; 1936) and served on the coaching staff at the University of Iowa (Iowa City; 1937). He served in the Marine Corps during World War II and after the war was a businessman in San Francisco. He was enshrined in the Pro Football Hall of Fame in 1963.

OTTO GRAHAM

(b. Dec. 6, 1921, Waukegan, Ill., U.S.—d. Dec. 17, 2003, Sarasota, Fla.)

Otto Graham is best remembered as the quarterback of the Cleveland Browns during a 10-year period in which they won 105 games, lost 17, and tied 5 in regular-season play and won 7 of 10 championship games.

Graham was an all-around athlete in high school. At Northwestern University (1941–43) he was named All-American in football (1943), and in 1944 he joined the U.S. Navy and trained as an aircraft pilot. The navy sent him to Colgate University, where he played basketball and was named an All-American.

Graham began his professional career in sports playing for the Rochester Royals in the National Basketball League. He then switched to football, playing for the Cleveland Browns. In college Graham had played tailback, which was the passing position in the single-wing formation used by Northwestern, but in Cleveland, where the T formation was favoured, he played quarterback. He led his league as a passer in six seasons; in the 1950 NFL championship game, he passed for four touchdowns; in the 1954 championship game, he passed for three and ran for three more. His career average yardage per pass of 8.63 yards was still an NFL record at the turn of the century, and his 10.55 yards per pass in 1955 was the third best single-season average in history. He was enshrined in the Pro Football Hall of Fame in 1965.

After retiring as a player, he was head coach and athletic director of the U.S. Coast Guard Academy (1959–66). He then served as general manager and coach of the NFL Washington Redskins (1966–68).

SID LUCKMAN

(b. Nov. 21, 1916, Brooklyn, N.Y., U.S.—d. July 5, 1998, North Miami Beach, Fla.)

During his 12 seasons (1939–50) in the NFL, Sid Luckman directed with exceptional success the revolutionary T-formation offense of the Chicago Bears. The forward-passing feats of Luckman and of his greatest adversary, quarterback Sammy Baugh of the Washington Redskins, terminated a long era in professional football in which offensive strategies were based largely on rushing from the single-wing formation.

As a collegian at Columbia University in New York City, Sidney Luckman was an important symbol for second- and third-generation American Jewish immigrants. Luckman was part of a remarkable generation of Jewish American athletes in basketball and boxing as well as football who used sport as an avenue to assimilation and success.

After graduating from Columbia in 1939, Luckman became the Bears' starting quarterback in his second NFL season, 1940. On December 8 of that year, he participated in the Bears' 73–0 victory over Washington in the most one-sided championship game in NFL history. With Luckman as quarterback, the Bears won additional championships in 1941, 1943, and 1946. For the 1943 season, he was named Most Valuable Player in the NFL. On November 14 of that year, he set a league record by passing for seven touchdowns in a single regular-season game, and on December 26 he established an NFL championship game record by throwing five touchdown passes as the Bears defeated Washington, 41–21. In average gain per pass attempt, he ranks second all-time for both a career (8.42) and a single season (10.86 in 1943).

After his retirement from active play, Luckman became a successful businessman in Chicago and a part-time assistant coach of the Bears. He was inducted into the Pro Football Hall of Fame in 1965.

CHUCK BEDNARIK

(b. May 1, 1925, Bethlehem, Pa., U.S.)

As a linebacker and centre for the Philadelphia Eagles in the 1950s and early '60s, Chuck Bednarik was the last player in league history to regularly participate in every play of an NFL game. Bednarik won two NFL championships (1949, 1960) with the Eagles.

An unexceptional football player in high school, Charles Phillip Bednarik enlisted in the U.S. Army Air Forces to fight in World War II soon after his graduation. As a waist gunner, he participated in 30 missions over Europe. Upon his return to the United States in 1945, Bednarik enrolled at the University of Pennsylvania and joined the football team. Blossoming quickly as a player, he earned consensus All-American honours at centre in his junior and senior seasons and in 1948 became the first offensive lineman to win the Maxwell Award as college football's most outstanding player. He was selected by the Eagles with the first overall pick of the 1949 NFL draft.

After watching the first two games of his rookie season from the bench, Bednarik began a streak of "iron man" play that saw him miss just one more game over the remainder of his 14 seasons in the league. "Concrete Charlie" was a standout on both sides of the ball—earning All-Pro honours at both centre and linebacker over the course of his career—but he became most famous for his hard-hitting plays on defense. Two of his tackles, both of which took place in 1960, have transcended the others to become part of NFL lore. In a November game against the New York Giants, Bednarik tackled star running back Frank Gifford so ferociously that Gifford was unable to return to the sport until 1962. A familiar photograph taken soon after the tackle shows Bednarik celebrating over a prone Gifford, a gesture that was perceived by some as cruel taunting but that was in fact a reaction not to Gifford's injury but to the fumble caused by the hit that sealed the win for Philadelphia. Bednarik's other memorable tackle came in the 1960 NFL championship: with the Eagles holding a 17–13 lead over the Green Bay Packers in the final seconds of the game, Bednarik alone stood between the end zone and Jim Taylor as the Packer fullback rumbled across the Eagles' 10-yard-line only to be brought down by Bednarik, who remained on top of Taylor until time ran out to clinch the championship for Philadelphia.

Bednarik retired after the 1962 season. He was named to eight career Pro Bowls and was inducted into the Pro Football Hall of Fame in 1967.

PAUL BROWN

(b. Sept. 7, 1908, Norwalk, Ohio, U.S. — d. Aug. 5, 1991, Cincinnati, Ohio)

A football coach known for his cerebral approach, innovative methods, iron rule, and cool demeanour, Paul Brown coached winning teams in high school, college, armed forces, and professional football.

Brown was an undersized quarterback at Miami University (Ohio), where he received a B.A. in education in 1930. He took a job as a teacher and football coach at Servern Prep School in 1930, compiling a 16–1–1 record in two seasons. From 1932 to 1940 he coached his high school alma mater at Massillon, Ohio, to several state championships and an 80–8–2 record. He became head coach at Ohio State University in 1941, where his teams went 18–9–1 and won the national collegiate championship in 1942. In 1944–45 he coached the team at Great Lakes Training Station, going 15–5–2.

While at Great Lakes he agreed to coach Cleveland's professional team, scheduled to begin play in 1946 in the new All-America Football Conference. Brown's popularity in Ohio was such that the team was named the Browns in his honour. During the AAFC's four seasons, the Browns won all four championships, with a total record 52–4–3. In 1950 the Browns moved to the NFL and immediately won the championship; they also won titles in 1954–55. Although Brown's teams continued to win, he was fired by Cleveland's owner Art Modell in 1962. After a six-year retirement, he returned to the NFL as founder and coach of an expansion team, the Cincinnati Bengals, and by the third year the team had won its division. He retired from coaching in 1975 but remained team president until his death. Overall his professional record was 222–102–9.

Among the unique methods and innovations for which Brown was famous were classroom study and notebooks for players (he even gave written tests), extensive use of film to grade player performance as well as to spot tendencies of opponents and his own team, the modern pass-blocking "pocket," the face mask, "messenger guards" so the coach could call plays, extensive use of "trap blocking" in the rushing attack, and sophisticated pass patterns. Many of his former players and assistants went on to coaching success in the NFL, including Hall of Famers Weeb Ewbank, Chuck Noll, Don Shula, and Bill Walsh. Brown was named to the Pro Football Hall of Fame in 1967.

ELROY HIRSCH

(b. June 17, 1923, Wausau, Wis., U.S.—d. Jan. 28, 2004, Madison, Wis.)

Elroy Hirsch was a football player, sports administrator, and actor who rose to fame as a collegiate star and who was a record-setting wide receiver with the Los Angeles Rams.

In 1942 Hirsch played halfback on the University of Wisconsin's football team and earned the nickname "Crazylegs" for an unorthodox running style that made him difficult to tackle. The following year he enlisted in the Marines and began officer training at the University of Michigan. There he became the school's only athlete to letter in four sports in the same year (football, basketball, baseball, and track). After World War II, Hirsch began playing professional football with the Chicago Rockets (1946–48) of the All-America Football Conference and endured several injury-plagued seasons before joining the NFL's Rams in 1949. Moved to the split end position, he became an integral part of the team's formidable offense, which relied heavily on the forward pass and featured a tandem of Hall of Fame quarterbacks Bob Waterfield and

Norm Van Brocklin. In the 1951 season Hirsch led the league in catches (66) and touchdown receptions (17) and set an NFL record (since broken) for receiving yards (1,495). His play helped the Rams win the NFL championship that year. Hirsch's immense popularity led to appearances in several movies during his playing days, including the auto-biographical *Crazylegs* (1953) and *Unchained* (1955).

In 1957 he retired from professional football with 387 career receptions for 7,029 yards and 60 touchdowns. He later served as athletic director (1969–87) at the University of Wisconsin and helped turn around the school's struggling sports program. Hirsch was inducted into the Pro Football Hall of Fame in 1968.

MARION MOTLEY

(b. June 5, 1920, Leesburg, Ga., U.S.—d. June 27, 1999, Cleveland, Ohio)

Marion Motley was an African American fullback who helped desegregate professional football in the 1940s during a career that earned him induction into the Pro Football Hall of Fame in 1968. Motley's bruising running style and exceptional blocking ability marked him as one of the sport's greatest players.

Motley was a fullback and linebacker for both South Carolina State University (Orangeburg) and the University of Nevada (Reno) before playing for the Great Lakes Naval Training Station during World War II. His coach there was Paul Brown, who later was named the first coach of the Cleveland Browns in the All-America Football Conference (AAFC). Motley signed with Cleveland as a fullback in 1946, breaking professional football's 13-year colour barrier along with three other players.

Motley, 6 feet 1 inch (1.85 metres) tall and weighing 238 pounds (108 kg), was the leading rusher in the four-year history of the AAFC, with 3,024 yards. The Cleveland Browns won every AAFC title and compiled a 47–4–3 regular-season record. Motley, who also contributed defensively, was an AAFC linebacker in each of his first three seasons.

When the Browns joined the NFL in 1950, Motley led the league with 810 yards, an average of 5.8 yards per carry, and was named to the All-Pro team. The Browns won the NFL title in 1950 and advanced to the title game in each of the next three seasons. Motley missed the 1954 season because of a knee injury. He finished his career with the Pittsburgh Steelers in 1955. In all, Motley totaled 4,720 rushing yards (a 5.7-yard average) and scored 31 touchdowns.

Motley's career has been overshadowed by later Browns fullback Jim Brown, who played in an era when the NFL attracted a broad national audience through television. However, Motley, using a similar combination of speed and power, was just as dominant during his career and was considered by many, including Coach Paul Brown, to have been the more complete player.

VINCE LOMBARDI

(b. June 11, 1913, Brooklyn, N.Y., U.S.—d. Sept. 3, 1970, Washington, D.C.)

In nine seasons (1959–67) as head coach of the previously moribund Green Bay Packers, Vince Lombardi led the team to five championships of the NFL and, in the last two seasons, to victory in the first two Super Bowl games. Over the course of his coaching career, the fiery Lombardi became a national symbol of single-minded determination to win.

At Fordham University, Vincent Thomas Lombardi was outstanding in the classroom as well as on the football field, where he was one of the group of linemen known as the "Seven Blocks of Granite." After completing his undergraduate education in business (1937), he studied law at

The 1966–67 Green Bay Packers lift head coach Vince Lombardi to celebrate their win over the Dallas Cowboys in the NFL championship game. Tony Tomsic/NFL/Getty Images

Fordham, briefly played semiprofessional football, and then entered high school football coaching (1939). Afterward he served as an assistant coach at Fordham (1947–48), at the U.S. Military Academy at West Point, New York (1949–53), and with the New York Giants of the NFL (1954–58).

Hired as head coach and general manager of the Packers in February 1959, Lombardi imposed an unusually strenuous regimen (some critics described it as spartan or fanatic) on his players, most of whom had been accustomed to defeat. The players who survived his relentless driving and gained his respect became deeply loyal to him. In his second year, Green Bay led the Western Conference of the NFL. The Packers subsequently won the league championship in 1961–62 and 1965–67 and defeated Kansas City and then Oakland in the Super Bowl games following the 1966 and 1967 seasons.

Unlike his chief rival, Tom Landry of the Dallas Cowboys, Lombardi excelled as a motivator rather than as an innovator. However, his teams were known for one signature play—the

Green Bay sweep. The play, which saw the ball carrier dash around the end escorted by a host of blockers, was copied by virtually every football team in the 1960s and '70s.

Retiring as coach, Lombardi served the Packers in 1968 as general manager. He then went to the Washington Redskins of the NFL as head coach, general manager, and part owner, and in 1969 he led the team to its first winning season in 14 years. He died shortly before the 1970 season.

During his most successful years in Green Bay and even after his death, Lombardi was widely esteemed for his views on the virtues of hard work and winning. Upon Lombardi's death, President Richard Nixon telegrammed condolences to Lombardi's widow, signing the message "The People." His personal philosophy is reflected in a celebrated quotation:

Winning is not a sometime thing: it's an all the time thing. You don't win once in a while; you don't do the right thing once in a while; you do them right all the time. Winning is a habit.

In 1971 the Super Bowl trophy was named in his memory. A year earlier the Lombardi Award, given annually to college football's top lineman, had been established. He was inducted into the Pro Football Hall of Fame in 1971.

JIM PARKER

(b. April 3, 1934, Macon, Ga., U.S. — d. July 18, 2005, Columbia, Md.)

During his 11-year career with the Baltimore Colts, Jim Parker established himself as one of the finest offensive linemen in NFL history.

James Thomas Parker played collegiate football at Ohio State University under legendary head coach Woody Hayes. He played on both the offensive and defensive sides of the ball, earning unanimous All-America honours and winning the Outland Trophy as the country's top lineman in 1956. Parker was selected by the Colts with the eighth overall choice in the 1957 NFL draft.

Parker became the team's starting left tackle, where the rookie was responsible for protecting the blind side of iconic quarterback Johnny Unitas. The 6-foot 3-inch (1.91-metre), 273-pound (124-kg) Parker readily took to the job, and in his second season in the league he earned the first of four consecutive Pro Bowl and All-Pro honours. "Jumbo Jim" anchored Baltimore's offensive lines that helped the team to NFL championships in 1958 and 1959. During the 1962 season, Parker switched to left guard and promptly earned dual All-Pro and Pro Bowl recognition at that position in each season through 1965. In 1973 he became the first full-time offensive lineman inducted into the Pro Football Hall of Fame, and he was named to the NFL's 75th Anniversary All-Time Team in 1994.

DICK LANE

(b. April 16, 1928, Austin, Texas, U.S.—d. Jan. 29, 2002, Austin)

Widely considered one of the greatest cornerbacks in NFL history, Dick Lane was named to seven Pro Bowls over the course of his career, and his 14 interceptions during the 1952 season are an NFL record.

Abandoned by his mother at three months of age, Richard Lane was raised by the woman who found him discarded in a trash bin. He briefly played football in junior college and then served in the U.S. Army for four years. At age 24, with no recent organized football experience outside of games played with his army base team, Lane walked into the offices of the Los Angeles Rams in 1952 and asked for a tryout. Lane impressed the Rams, who had initially tried him at offensive end before switching him to the defensive backfield, and he was offered a spot on the team. He earned a starting role as a rookie and proceeded to take the league by storm, intercepting a record 14 passes in just 12 games.

Standing 6 feet 1 inch (1.85 metres) tall and weighing around 200 pounds (91 kg), Lane was larger than most of the receivers he covered, and he quickly gained a reputation as a ferocious tackler. His signature tackle, which involved wrapping his arms around an opponent's neck and wrestling him to the ground, became known as the "Night Train Necktie" (after Lane's well-known "Night Train" nickname) and was eventually banned by the league for being too dangerous. After two years with the Rams, Lane was traded to the Chicago Cardinals in 1954. In his first season in Chicago, he again led the NFL in interceptions (with 10) and also earned the first of seven career Pro Bowl honours. He was dealt to the Detroit Lions in 1960 and retired from the sport after the 1965 season.

After his retirement, Lane was the road manager for comedian Redd Foxx for a short time, and he had coaching stints at Central State University in Wilberforce, Ohio, and Southern University in Baton Rouge, La. He was briefly married to renowned rhythm-and-blues singer Dinah Washington until her death in 1963. Lane was inducted into the Pro Football Hall of Fame in 1974 and was chosen as one of four cornerbacks on the NFL's 75th anniversary team in 1994.

GALE SAYERS

(b. May 30, 1943, Wichita, Kan., U.S.)

In 1977 Gale Sayers became the youngest player ever voted into the Pro Football Hall of Fame. Though knee injuries shortened his career, Sayers showed in his seven seasons that he was one of the most elusive running backs in the history of the NFL.

Sayers grew up in Omaha, Neb., where he was a star running back and record-setting long jumper in high school. He first gained national attention as a two-time All-American (1963–64) at the University of Kansas. Sayers was drafted by the Chicago Bears in 1965, and in his first season he amassed 2,272 combined rushing, receiving, and kick-return yards, as well as 22 touchdowns, a record for a rookie. That year, in a game against the San Francisco 49ers, he tied an NFL record by scoring six touchdowns in a single game. Not surprisingly, he was named Rookie of the Year in 1965. He twice led the league in rushing (1966, 1969), was named All-Pro five years in a row (1965–69), and has the best career kickoff-return average in the NFL (30.6 yards per return). Sayers was known for his distinctive long-legged running style, which was highlighted by his ability to make explosive cutbacks at nearly full speed as he dodged defenders.

A series of significant knee injuries forced Sayers to retire at age 29 before the 1972 NFL season. He later served as assistant athletic director at the University of Kansas (1972–76) and as athletic director at Southern Illinois University (1976–81). In 1984 Sayers founded a successful computer supplies business. His close friendship with fellow Bears halfback Brian Piccolo, who died of cancer in 1970, was depicted in the 1971 television movie *Brian's Song*. Sayers cowrote two autobiographies, *I Am Third* (with Al Silverman; 1970) and *Sayers: My Life and Times* (with Fred Mitchell; 2007).

DICK BUTKUS

(b. Dec. 9, 1942, Chicago, Ill., U.S.)

As middle linebacker for the Chicago Bears, Dick Butkus was the dominant defensive player of his era. He was exceptionally large for a linebacker playing in the 1960s (6 feet 3 inches [1.9 metres] and 245 pounds [111 kg]) and had a reputation for relentless pursuit and ferocious tackling.

Richard Marvin Butkus played both fullback and linebacker at Chicago Vocational High School. As a middle linebacker at the University of Illinois (1962–64), he earned consensus All-America honours in 1963 and 1964, his senior season, when he also finished third in the voting for the Heisman Trophy (an exceptional result for a defensive player).

Butkus was selected by the Bears and by the Denver Broncos in the first round of the NFL and the AFL draft, respectively. He signed with his hometown team, and in his first year with the Bears (1965) he intercepted five passes and was selected for the first of eight consecutive Pro Bowls. Butkus, who led the Bears in tackles in each of his first eight seasons in the league, was famous for his ability to strip the ball during a tackle. In a career shortened by injuries, he accumulated 1,020 tackles, 22 interceptions, and 27 fumble recoveries, the last an NFL record for a defensive player at the time of his retirement.

After retiring in 1973, Butkus acted on television and in films. A five-time first-team All-Pro selection, he was elected to the Pro Football Hall of Fame in 1979 and in 1994 was named to the NFL's 75th Anniversary All-Time Team. Since 1985 the Downtown Athletic Club of Orlando (Fla.) has awarded the Butkus Trophy to the outstanding collegiate linebacker of the year.

MERLIN OLSEN

(b. Sept. 15, 1940, Logan, Utah—d. March 11, 2010, Duarte, Calif.)

Merlin Olsen was one of the most extraordinary defensive linemen in NFL history.

Olsen, a 6-foott 5-inch (1.9-metre) tackle, was a consensus All-American in his senior season at Utah State University, where he helped lead the unheralded program to national prominence as a member of an outstanding defensive unit. He was drafted by the NFL's Los Angeles Rams in 1962 and was instantly inserted into the team's starting lineup. Though the Rams won only one game in the 1962 season, Olsen was named the NFL Rookie of the Year. A ferocious run-stuffer, he made up a part of the formidable Rams defensive line that was heralded as the "Fearsome Foursome" and dominated the NFL throughout the remainder of the 1960s. For every year but his final one with the Rams, Olsen was voted to the Pro Bowl. He retired in 1976 as the Rams' all-time leader in tackles, with a career 915.

Olsen was inducted into the College Football Hall of Fame in 1980 and the Pro Football Hall of Fame in 1982. In 1994 he was named to the NFL's 75th Anniversary All-Time Team. Olsen's brothers Phil and Orrin also played in the NFL; Phil and Merlin played together from 1971 to 1974.

After leaving the Rams, Olsen served as an NFL commentator, television spokesperson, and TV actor, best known for his recurring role as Jonathan Garvey (1977–81) on *Little House on the Prairie*, as the star of *Father Murphy* (1981–83), and as Aaron Miller in the short-lived *Aaron's Way* (1988).

O.J. SIMPSON

(b. July 9, 1947, San Francisco, Calif., U.S.)

A premier collegiate and professional running back known for his speed and elusiveness, O.J. Simpson is arguably better known for his trial on murder charges in 1995, which was one of the most celebrated criminal trials in American history.

Orenthal James Simpson played football at Galileo High School in San Francisco, first as a tackle and then as a fullback. He attended San Francisco City College (1965–66) to achieve a scholastic record that allowed him to play at the University of Southern California (USC), where he set team records for yards gained by rushing in 1967 (1,415 yards) and 1968 (1,709 yards). He was named All-American (1967–68), played in two Rose Bowl games, and won the Heisman Trophy as the best collegiate player of the season (1968). At USC he was also a member of a world-record-setting 440-yard relay team.

Simpson, who was often called "Juice" because of his energetic runs and because his initials could stand for "orange juice," was the number one draft choice of the AFL Buffalo Bills in 1969. The following year the AFL merged with the NFL. The Bills were members of the AFC of the NFL when Simpson set a single-season record for yards gained rushing (2,003) in 1973. The Bills were never a contending team during his stay, but he was a great box-office draw. Injuries to his knees prompted the Bills to trade him in 1978 to the San Francisco 49ers, but he retired after the 1979 season. His 1975 record of most touchdowns scored in a season (23) stood until 1983, and his 1973 season rushing record for most yards gained lasted until 1984, when it was broken by Eric Dickerson. Simpson led the AFC in rushing yardage four times (1972–73, 1975–76). His career total yards gained (11,236) was second in the all-time rankings at the time of his retirement. He was inducted into the Pro Football Hall of Fame in 1985.

After retiring from football, Simpson became a film and television actor and sports commentator. On June 12, 1994, his ex-wife Nicole Brown Simpson and her friend Ronald Goldman were stabbed to death outside her home in Los Angeles. Simpson was arrested and charged with the two murders on June 17. He pleaded not guilty and

O.J. Simpson with U.S. soldiers, 1990. Gerald Johnson/U.S. Department of Defense

hired a team of prominent lawyers to handle his defense. His lengthy nationally televised trial became the focus of unprecedented media scrutiny. A jury acquitted Simpson of the murder charges on Oct. 3, 1995. In a separate civil trial decision in 1997, he was found liable for the deaths of his ex-wife and Goldman and was ordered to pay $33.5 million in damages to the families. Simpson later collaborated (with Pablo F. Fenjves) on *If I Did It*, in which he hypothesized about how he would have committed the murders. Public outrage prevented its initial publication in 2006, but a bankruptcy court subsequently awarded the book's rights to the Goldman family, who released the work in 2007.

Later that year, Simpson was arrested after he and several other men entered a Las Vegas hotel room and took memorabilia items that Simpson claimed had been stolen from him. The incident resulted in Simpson being charged with a number of crimes, including armed robbery and kidnapping. On Oct. 3, 2008, a jury found him guilty of all charges. He was later sentenced to a minimum of nine years in prison, with a possible maximum sentence of 33 years.

ROGER STAUBACH

(b. Feb. 5, 1942, Cincinnati, Ohio, U.S.)

A collegiate and professional quarterback, Roger Staubach was an important factor in the establishment of the Dallas Cowboys as a dominant team in the 1970s.

Staubach played college football at the U.S. Naval Academy (1962–65), where as a quarterback he gained 4,253 yards (3,571 yards by passing) and scored 18 touchdowns. He was named All-American and won the Heisman Trophy as the best collegiate player in 1963. He served in the U.S. Navy (1965–69) following graduation from the academy.

During Staubach's career with the Cowboys (1969–79), they were in the playoffs every year but one (1974) and played in four Super Bowl games, winning in the 1971 and 1977 seasons. Staubach led the league in passer rating in four seasons (1971, 1973, 1978–79). In his career Staubach, known as "Captain Comeback," rallied the Cowboys to victory in 14 games in which, with two minutes to play, they were either tied or losing. His wholesome image and professional demeanour, together with those of his coach, Tom Landry, were a major part of the Cowboy's characterization as "America's Team" in the 1970s. Staubach announced his retirement from football in 1979 and was briefly a sports announcer. He was inducted into the Pro Football Hall of Fame in 1985.

MIKE DITKA

(b. Oct. 18, 1939, Carnegie, Pa., U.S.)

In the 1960s and early '70s Mike Ditka proved himself one of professional football's greatest tight ends, using his talent for catching passes to revolutionize his position. After retiring as a player, Ditka embarked on a successful coaching career, the highlight of which came in 1986, when he led the Chicago Bears to a Super Bowl victory.

Michael Keller Ditka attended the University of Pittsburgh, where he was named first-team All-American in 1960. A first-round draft selection by the Bears, Ditka earned NFL Rookie of the Year honours in 1961. In each of his first five seasons in Chicago, he was chosen for the Pro Bowl, and he helped the Bears capture the 1963 NFL championship. Ditka also played for the Philadelphia Eagles in 1967–68 and then for the Dallas Cowboys in 1969–72. "Iron

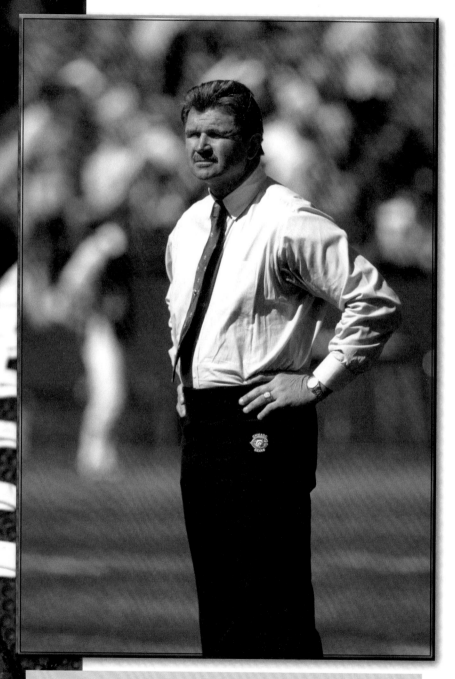

Chicago Bears head Coach Mike Ditka on the sidelines during a game against the San Francisco 49ers in 1985. George Rose/Getty Images

Mike" caught 30 passes during the 1971 season en route to helping the Cowboys win their first Super Bowl title the following January. He retired after the 1972 season. Over the course of his playing career, Ditka made 427 receptions, gained 5,812 yards, and scored 43 touchdowns. At the time, these were phenomenal totals for a tight end, which hitherto had been viewed primarily as a blocking position.

Ditka served as an assistant coach for the Cowboys from 1973 to 1981, during which time the team captured its second Super Bowl title, in 1978. He became head coach of the Bears in 1982. His tenure as coach in Chicago was marked by some of the franchise's greatest moments: six NFC Central Division titles, three appearances in the NFC title game, and a Super Bowl victory. His wildly popular 1985 team, which included legendary running back Walter Payton and one of the best defenses in NFL history, lost only a single game during the regular season and routed the New England Patriots by a score of 46–10 in Super Bowl XX. Ditka thus became one of only two men to experience Super Bowl wins as a player, as an assistant coach, and as a head coach. In both 1985 and 1988 Ditka was voted the NFL Coach of the Year.

The Bears' play fell off in 1992, and Ditka was let go at the end of the season. He returned to the NFL as head coach of the New Orleans Saints in 1997. He accumulated a record of 15–33 in three disappointing seasons with the Saints before being fired. In 2001 Ditka joined the ownership of the Chicago Rush, a member of the Arena Football League. He also worked frequently as a commentator on NFL telecasts and as a spokesperson for a vast number of products. *Ditka: An Autobiography*, cowritten by Don Pierson, appeared in 1986. In 1988 Ditka was inducted into the Pro Football Hall of Fame, the first tight end ever to receive the honour. In 1994 Ditka was one of two tight ends named to the NFL's 75th Anniversary All-Time Team.

ALAN PAGE

(b. Aug. 7, 1945, Canton, Ohio, U.S.)

In 1971 Alan Page became the first defensive player to win the NFL's Most Valuable Player award.

At the University of Notre Dame (1963–67), Page played defensive end for the 1966 national championship team, receiving All-America honours. After graduating he was drafted by the Minnesota Vikings of the NFL. With the Vikings, he played defensive tackle and joined with Jim Marshall, Carl Eller, and Gary Larsen to form the legendary defensive line known as the "Purple People-Eaters." He was named Rookie of the Year in 1967.

With the Vikings, Page appeared in four Super Bowls and was named All-Pro every year from 1970 to 1977. Weighing 240 pounds (109 kg), he was relatively small for a lineman, yet he was so uncommonly quick that he was often across the line of scrimmage before his opponents could stop him. In 1971, his best season, he recorded 109 tackles, 35 assists, 10 quarterback sacks, and 3 safeties.

In the middle of his career, Page took up running and even competed in marathons. The training led to a loss of weight to below 220 pounds (100 kg), however, and he was released by the Vikings in 1978. He played the final four years of his career with the Chicago Bears. The unofficial record shows that, in his 15 years of professional football, Page never missed a game, starting in 236 contests. He held a career record for highest number of safeties and blocked kicks. Page was inducted into the Pro Football Hall of Fame in 1988.

During his playing days, Page entered law school and in 1978 earned a law degree from the University of Minnesota. He went into private practice in 1979 and then joined the Minnesota attorney general's office in 1985.

In 1993 he became an associate justice of the Minnesota Supreme Court.

TERRY BRADSHAW

(b. Sept. 2, 1948, Shreveport, La., U.S.)

Quarterback Terry Bradshaw led the Pittsburgh Steelers to four Super Bowl championships (1975, 1976, 1979, 1980).

A highly prized collegiate football recruit coming out of high school, Terry Paxton Bradshaw shunned traditional powerhouse Louisiana State University to attend the smaller Louisiana Tech University in Ruston, which was only about 70 miles (113 km) from his hometown. He broke all of the major school passing records in his four years at Louisiana Tech and was selected by the Steelers with the first overall selection of the 1970 NFL draft. Bradshaw became the team's full-time starting quarterback in his second season in Pittsburgh, and in 1972 he led the team to the first of eight consecutive play-off appearances. While the well-balanced team was one of the most successful in the league, Bradshaw struggled with his passing accuracy and was demoted to backup quarterback early in the 1974 season. He played his way back into the starting lineup over the course of the season and led the Steelers to their first Super Bowl title the following January.

Entrenched as the Steelers' quarterback, Bradshaw guided the team to a second consecutive championship in 1976. In 1978 he threw a league-high 28 touchdown passes and was named the NFL's Most Valuable Player (MVP). In the subsequent postseason, he ran an efficient offense that averaged 34 points per game, and the Steelers garnered another Super Bowl victory (with Bradshaw earning game MVP honours). The team again repeated as champions in 1980, and Bradshaw was once more named Super Bowl

MVP for his efforts. He retired after the 1983 season and was inducted into the Pro Football Hall of Fame in 1989.

After retiring as a player, Bradshaw became a prominent television football analyst. In addition, he acted in a number of telelvision programs and films, and he had some success as a gospel and country music singer. His book *It's Only a Game* (2001; cowritten with David Fisher) chronicles his life from his early years to his post-football exploits.

FRANCO HARRIS

(b. March 7, 1950, Fort Dix, N.J., U.S.)

Running back Franco Harris was a member of four Super Bowl–winning teams (1975, 1976, 1979, 1980) as a Pittsburgh Steeler and is best known for having taken part in arguably the most famous play in NFL history, "the Immaculate Reception."

Harris was a star in baseball, basketball, and football during high school, and he earned a football scholarship to Pennsylvania State University (Penn State) in 1968. At Penn State he was often overshadowed by fellow running back Lydell Mitchell, an All-American, but Steelers scouts still saw enough in Harris's play to draft him with the 13th overall selection of the 1972 NFL draft. Having rushed for 1,055 yards and scored 10 touchdowns in his first year in the league, he was named Offensive Rookie of the Year and chosen for the first of nine consecutive Pro Bowls. The Steelers qualified for the play-offs for the first time in 25 years that season, and their first-round game against the Oakland Raiders was highlighted by Harris's game-winning shoestring catch that came to be know as the Immaculate Reception. The play occurred with 22 seconds remaining in the game and the Steelers trailing

7–6. On fourth-and-10 from the Steelers' 40-yard line, Pittsburgh's quarterback, Terry Bradshaw, threw a pass that was deflected toward the ground by a Raider defender before Harris appeared seemingly out of nowhere to snatch the ball and run into the end zone. While the play proved controversial—some observers maintain that the ball either hit the ground before Harris caught it or was deflected by another Pittsburgh player instead of the Oakland defender, which was illegal at the time—it was nevertheless ruled a touchdown, and the Steelers ultimately won the game.

In addition to his Pro Bowl streak, Harris helped the Steelers to eight straight play-off berths from 1972, four of which resulted in Super Bowl titles. He was named Most Valuable Player of Super Bowl IX (1975) after rushing for 158 yards against a stout Minnesota Vikings defense. At 6 feet 2 inches (1.88 metres) and 230 pounds (104 kg), he was a large running back, but he was often criticized for being "soft" because of his tendency to avoid contact that he deemed unnecessary by running out of bounds. However, his cautious running style led to a long career; he played 12 seasons with the Steelers and one more with the Seattle Seahawks. At the time of his retirement in 1984, he had the third highest career rushing yardage total in NFL history. Harris was inducted into the Pro Football Hall of Fame in 1990.

TOM LANDRY

(b. Sept. 11, 1924, Mission, Texas, U.S.—d. Feb. 12, 2000, Dallas, Texas)

Tom Landry was a football coach best known for his tenure with the Dallas Cowboys from 1960 to 1989. He molded the Cowboys into a dominant team from the late 1960s to the early '80s.

Thomas Wade Landry began his professional career as a player with the All-America Football Conference New York Yankees (1949) and moved to the NFL New York Giants (1950–55) as a cornerback. He was a player-coach in 1954–55, and, as an assistant coach in charge of defense through the 1959 season, his 4–3 alignment revolutionized defensive play, making it a glamorous part of the game.

Landry became coach of the newly formed Cowboys team in 1960, and in his first season they won no games, lost 11, and tied 1. Losing seasons continued for the team through 1964. The Cowboys then went on to 20 consecutive winning seasons. They competed in 2 NFL championship games, 10 NFC championship games, and 5 Super Bowls, losing 3 of them (1971, 1976, and 1979) and winning 2 (1972 and 1978). While his teams were celebrated for their innovative play (the Cowboys revived the shotgun formation and pioneered situational substitutions) and computer-aided efficiency, Landry himself was known for his bland demeanour, his conservative dress (he was rarely seen without a sport coat and a fedora) on the sidelines, and, away from football, his religious piety. His overall record was 270 wins, 178 losses, and 6 ties, a .601 winning percentage.

After several consecutive losing seasons, Landry was dismissed as coach of the Cowboys in 1989, when the team was sold to a new owner. In 1990 he was elected to the Pro Football Hall of Fame.

CHAPTER 6
SELECTED PRO FOOTBALL HALL OF FAMERS, 1991 THROUGH THE PRESENT

For the most part, the individuals profiled in this chapter rose to prominence in the 1980s and '90s—an era when cable and satellite television helped speed the tremendous growth in popularity of the sport and when the NFL began to become the global business colossus it is today. As a result, players such as Walter Payton, Lawrence Taylor, Joe Montana, Dan Marino, and Jerry Rice have some of the most famous faces of all American athletes—a testament to just how prevalent the American brand of football has become, The following biographies of these players and more are arranged in order of year of induction into the Hall of Fame.

JOHN HANNAH

(b. April 4, 1951, Canton, Ga., U.S.)

John Hannah's combination of size, strength, and athleticism helped him redefine the guard position. Hannah played for the New England Patriots from 1973 to 1985 and was named All-Pro on seven occasions.

Hannah was a notable multisport athlete in high school. In addition to being a star on the football team, he won the national heavyweight prep wrestling championship in 1967. He played collegiate football at the University of Alabama, where he was a three-year starter on the offensive line and a consensus All-American in his senior season. Hannah was chosen by the Patriots with the fourth overall selection of the 1973 NFL draft.

Hannah was immediately inserted in the starting lineup upon joining the Patriots. His 6-foot 2-inch (1.88-metre), 265-pound (120-kg) frame was considered to be exceptionally large at that time in football history, and his size was augmented by remarkable quickness and agility that made Hannah especially effective when blocking in space on runs downfield and when pulling to engage a defensive player at the end of the line. Hannah's spectacular run blocking was a major factor in the Patriots' setting the NFL single-season team rushing record by piling up 3,165 yards in 1978. He was also a standout pass blocker and is regarded by many observers as the greatest interior offensive lineman in league history.

After helping the Patriots franchise make its first Super Bowl appearance in January 1986 (a loss to the Chicago Bears), Hannah retired from the sport. He then became an investment banker and later launched a Christian-oriented corporate training company. A nine-time career Pro Bowl honoree, Hannah was elected to the Pro Football Hall of Fame in 1991 and was named to the NFL's 75th Anniversary All-Time Team in 1994.

AL DAVIS

(b. July 4, 1929, Brockton, Mass., U.S.)

As commissioner of the AFL, Al Davis was a key actor in the merger of the AFL with the NFL. Davis has been either a part owner or principal owner of the Oakland Raiders football franchise since 1966.

Allen Davis was raised in Brooklyn, N.Y., where his disciplinarian parents instilled a highly competitive disposition in him. After graduating from Syracuse University in 1950, he talked his way—despite having had no previous coaching experience—into an assistant coach position at Adelphi College (now Adelphi University), which he then parlayed into a job as the head coach of the U.S. Army football team based at Fort Belvoir, Va., in 1952. He made his first foray into the NFL in 1954 as a scout for the Baltimore (now Indianapolis) Colts before returning to college football as an assistant coach at the Citadel and at the University of Southern California.

In 1960 Davis was hired as an assistant coach for the AFL's Los Angeles (later San Diego) Chargers, and three years later he became the head coach and general manager of the Oakland Raiders. In his first season he led the Raiders to a 10–4 record one year after the team had finished 1–13, and he was named the AFL's Coach of the Year. He became AFL commissioner in April 1966, and, per Davis's instructions, AFL teams immediately began signing away some of the NFL's star players. Davis believed that the AFL was a better product than the NFL and could stand on its own, and his aggressive approach forced the NFL to recognize the growing influence of the younger league. Unbeknownst to Davis, the NFL and a number of AFL owners agreed to merge the two leagues just two months after Davis's reign as commissioner began. Unhappy with the merged league, he resigned his post in July 1966 and became the Raiders' director of football operations as well as a minority owner of the franchise.

Davis quickly built the Raiders into one of the most dominant teams in professional football. The team won the AFL title in the second season of his return and qualified for the play-offs in 10 of his first 12 years of guiding the team, including a Super Bowl victory in 1977. Davis bought out (and, in some cases, forced out) the other members of the Raiders' ownership group over the course of the early 1970s until he gained sole control over the team in 1976. Davis's impact on the team's on-field production was mirrored by the effect he had on the Raiders' lasting reputation. He coined the phrase "Just win, baby," which came to serve as a rationale for the notoriously rough— and sometimes illegal—play that was a hallmark of the team in the '70s. In addition, Davis's tendency to dress in all black, which he complemented with dark sunglasses, was in keeping with the Raiders' "bad boy" image.

In 1980, despite the fact that the Raiders had enjoyed a 12-year streak of home sellouts dating from 1968, Davis announced that he was moving the team to Los Angeles because he was unhappy with the conditions of the Raiders' home stadium. The city of Oakland, the NFL, and Davis then entered into a prolonged legal battle over the fate of the team. Despite the off-field turmoil, the Raiders captured a second Super Bowl championship in 1981. In 1982 Davis won a landmark antitrust lawsuit against the NFL, and the Raiders relocated to southern California. The team won the Super Bowl in its second season in its new home, but Davis once again became disenchanted with the quality of his stadium over time, and he returned the Raiders to Oakland in 1995.

After the glory years of the Raiders in the 1970s and early '80s faded, Davis's reputation among football fans began to diminish. The team was one of the worst in the league in the early years of the 21st century, and Davis became known for habitual poor personnel moves and public clashes with players and coaches, which often stemmed from his tendency to assert undue influence over on-field decisions from his front-office position. However, he did make some significant personnel moves at this time, including the hiring of Art Shell as head coach in 1989, which made Shell the first African American head coach in the modern era of the NFL. Davis was inducted into the Pro Football Hall of Fame in 1992.

WALTER PAYTON

(b. July 25, 1954, Columbia, Miss., U.S.—d. Nov. 1, 1999, Barrington, Ill.)

Walter Payton's productivity and durability made him one of the game's greatest running backs. He retired in 1987 as the leading rusher in the history of the NFL, a title he held until 2002, when he was surpassed by Emmitt Smith.

Payton played football in high school and at Jackson State University in Mississippi. It was during his college years that he gained the nickname "Sweetness" for his affable personality and graceful athleticism. In addition to his role as starting running back, he was also an occasional kicker at Jackson State, and his four-year total of 464 points was a National Collegiate Athletic Association record. He was drafted by the Chicago Bears with the fourth overall selection of the 1975 NFL draft. Payton was named to the first of nine career Pro Bowls in his second season, and in 1977 he won the league's Most Valuable Player award after leading the NFL in rushing yards (1,852; a franchise record) and rushing touchdowns (14). In the 1985 season he helped the Bears post a 15–1 record and win the franchise's first Super Bowl title the following January. He retired after the 1987 season.

Besides being an outstanding rusher, Payton was a capable blocker, pass receiver, and even passer. He was best known, however, for his pinball running style, in which he often bounced off would-be tacklers. His rigorous off-season training regimen contributed to his durability; he started in more than 180 consecutive games in his career. Payton set NFL records—all of which have since been broken—for

When Walter Payton retired from football in 1987 he held a number of records, including that of leading rusher in NFL history. Rogers Photo Archive/ Getty Images

total career rushing yardage (16,726 yards), most combined career yards from scrimmage (rushing and pass receiving, 21,264 yards), most seasons with 1,000 or more yards rushing (10), most yards gained in a single game (275 yards), most games with 100 or more yards gained in a career (77), and most career touchdowns earned by rushing (110).

Payton was inducted into the Pro Football Hall of Fame in 1993, and in 1994 he was named to the NFL's 75th Anniversary All-Time Team. The Walter Payton Award, established in 1987, is presented annually to the top player in the Football Championship Subdivision of college football. During his final year of life, while suffering from a rare liver disease, Payton was credited with awakening national interest in organ donation.

TONY DORSETT

(b. April 7, 1954, Rochester, Pa., U.S.)

Tony Dorsett is widely considered one of the best running backs in the sport's history.

A four-year starter and three-time All-American at the University of Pittsburgh, Anthony Drew Dorsett set collegiate records for the most 100-yard rushing performances in a season (11) and a career (33), though both have since been broken. He was the first back in the history of the National Collegiate Athletic Association to rush for 1,000 yards or more in all four years of his college career, and the first to surpass 1,500 yards three times. After rushing for 1,948 yards in his senior season, Dorsett won college football's most prestigious award, the Heisman Trophy, in 1976. He finished his collegiate career by establishing a new four-year rushing record of 6,082 total yards that stood until 1998.

The Dallas Cowboys selected Dorsett with the second overall selection in the 1977 NFL draft. He had little trouble adjusting to the professional game, winning the 1977 NFL Rookie of the Year award. Dorsett went on to establish himself as one of the NFL's most prolific runners, collecting at least 1,000 yards in eight of his first nine seasons, falling short only in the strike-shortened campaign of 1982. His efforts helped lead the Cowboys to five NFC championship games and two Super Bowls, including a Super Bowl title in 1978.

Dorsett's consistently outstanding statistics were a testament to his durability and versatility. He was chosen to play in the Pro Bowl four times (1978, 1981–83) and was named first-team All-Pro in 1981.

Dorsett retired in 1988 after spending his final professional season with the Denver Broncos. At the time of his retirement, he was the NFL's second leading rusher of all time with 12,739 career yards. In his 12-year career, he accumulated 16,293 total yards (rushing and receiving) and scored 90 touchdowns.

After his playing days ended, Dorsett became a successful businessman. He was inducted into both the College Football Hall of Fame and the Pro Football Hall of Fame in 1994.

STEVE LARGENT

(b. Sept. 28, 1954, Tulsa, Okla., U.S.)

Considered one of the greatest wide receivers of all time, Steve Largent retired from the sport as the owner of all of the major career NFL receiving records.

Although he was a standout high school football player and all-around athlete, Stephen Michael Largent was not heavily recruited by college scouts, so he enrolled at the lesser-known University of Tulsa in his hometown. After graduating in 1976 following one of the most outstanding careers in the history of Tulsa's football program, Largent was selected by the Houston Oilers in the NFL draft. He never appeared in a Houston uniform, however, as the Oilers dealt him to the Seattle Seahawks in a preseason trade.

Largent had an immediate influence with the Seahawks, catching 54 passes in his rookie season. What made him a great receiver was his excellent hands, the intelligence and ability to run crisp routes that got him into the open, and the strength to gain extra yards after catching the ball. It was this extra effort that earned the respect and admiration of opponents and fans alike. Largent's incredible durability—he missed only four games due to injury in his first 13 seasons—made him an institution at the wide receiver position.

Over the course of his 14 seasons, Largent raised the bar by which other receivers were measured. He caught 70 or more passes six times and caught at least 50 in 10 seasons. He set a record by catching at least one pass in 177 straight games (broken in 1994) and led the NFL in receiving twice (1979 and 1985). He recorded 819 pass receptions for 13,089 total receiving yards and collected 100 receiving touchdowns, all of which were NFL records that have since been broken. Largent became a perennial AFC Pro Bowl team member, making the squad seven times. He was inducted into the Pro Football Hall of Fame in 1995.

Largent retired from football in 1989 after spending his entire career in Seattle. He worked as a marketing consultant for the Sara Lee Corporation from 1991 to 1994 and, after a lifetime of community involvement and interest in politics, decided to run for national office. In 1994 Largent was elected to the U.S. House of Representatives from Oklahoma's first district. He was reelected on three occasions before leaving his office to mount an unsuccessful bid for the Oklahoma governorship in 2002. In 2003 he became the president of a cellular communications lobbying group.

DON SHULA

(b. Jan. 4, 1930, Grand River, Ohio, U.S.)

As a head football coach, notably of the Miami Dolphins from 1970 to 1995, Don Shula won more games than any other NFL coach.

At Harvey High School (Painesville, Ohio) Donald Francis Shula was an all-around athlete, playing baseball and basketball as well as football, and at John Carroll University (JCU; Cleveland, Ohio) he played halfback and defensive back. He received his B.S. degree in 1951 from JCU and an M.A. in physical education in 1953 from Western Reserve University (now Case Western Reserve University, in Cleveland).

Shula played professionally for the Cleveland Browns (1951–52), the Baltimore Colts (1953–56), and the Washington Redskins (1957). He began coaching in 1958 as an assistant at the University of Virginia and, the following year, at the University of Kentucky. He was defensive backfield coach for the Detroit Lions (1960–62) before becoming head coach of the Baltimore Colts in 1963. His Baltimore teams won division championships in 1964 and 1968; the 1968 team went on to capture the NFL championship but lost the Super Bowl. Overall, the Colts under Shula won 71 games, lost 23, and tied 4 in seven regular seasons.

After becoming coach of the Miami Dolphins in 1970, he became the first NFL coach to win 100 regular-season games in 10 seasons (1963–72). In 1971 Miami won the conference championship but lost the Super Bowl. The Dolphins in the 1972 season became the first team to go undefeated through their entire schedule and the

Don Shula coaching the Miami Dolphins, 1996. Rhona Wise/AFP/
Getty Images

play-offs, culminating with a win in the Super Bowl. The team won a second Super Bowl the following season. Shula again guided the Dolphins to the Super Bowl following the 1983 and 1985 seasons, but the team lost both times. On Nov. 14, 1993, Shula scored his 325th career victory, breaking George Halas's record. He retired after the 1995 season with a record of 347–173–6 (.665), including play-off games. He was enshrined in the Pro Football Hall of Fame in 1997.

ANTHONY MUÑOZ

(b. Aug. 19, 1958, Ontario, Calif., U.S.)

Anthony Muñoz is widely regarded as the greatest offensive lineman in the history of the NFL.

Muñoz attended the University of Southern California (USC), where he pitched for the school's national-championship-winning baseball team during his sophomore year and was a two-time All-American (1978–79) in football. Despite concerns over the three knee surgeries he had undergone during his four years at USC, he was chosen by the Cincinnati Bengals with the third overall selection of the 1980 NFL draft and was inserted into the team's starting lineup for the first game of his rookie season.

The 6-foot 6-inch (1.98-metre), 280-pound (127-kg) Muñoz was far more athletic and nimble than his linemen peers. As the passing game increased in prominence in the NFL during the 1970s, his combination of size and quickness helped redefine the left tackle position as an agile protector of the quarterback's blind side. Muñoz earned Pro Bowl and All-Pro honours in his second season as the Bengals advanced to their first Super Bowl appearance in franchise history, a loss to the San Francisco 49ers. He was selected to the Pro Bowl in each season through 1991, and was named first-team All-Pro eight additional times over the course of his career. Muñoz and the Bengals again faced the 49ers in the Super Bowl in 1989, but they were once more left without a championship. He briefly retired after the 1992 season. His attempted comeback with the Tampa Bay Buccaneers in 1993 ended with a preseason shoulder injury, after which Muñoz stepped away from the game for good. In 1994 he was named to the NFL's 75th Anniversary All-Time Team, and in 1998 he became the first Bengal to be inducted into the Pro Football Hall of Fame.

MIKE SINGLETARY

(b. Oct. 9, 1958, Houston, Texas, U.S.)

A middle linebacker for the Chicago Bears from 1981 to 1992, the remarkably durable Mike Singletary played nearly every down and missed only two games in his 12-year career.

Michael Singletary's father was an assistant minister whose strict adherence to rigid church doctrine prevented his son from playing football until he reached junior high. Although he was told that he was too small for the game, Singletary discovered a talent for delivering hard, decisive hits to ball carriers while playing linebacker for his high school team. In college at Baylor University, he averaged 15 tackles a game and was consensus All-American and Southwest Conference Player of the Year in both 1979 and 1980. Despite standing only 5 feet 11 inches (1.8 metres) tall, "Samurai Mike" established a reputation for hitting hard enough to break helmets—both his own and his opponents'—with his ferocious tackles.

Singletary was drafted by the Bears in the second round of the 1981 NFL draft. Despite not starting for the first seven games of the 1981 season, he still managed to earn NFL all-rookie team honours. Singletary secured his hold on the middle linebacker position from 1982 and, beginning in his breakthrough season of 1983, Singletary was the Bears' first or second leading tackler in each of his last 10 seasons. He played in 10 consecutive Pro Bowls from 1983 through 1992 and was first-team All-Pro in seven of those seasons. He was the NFL's Defensive Player of the Year in 1985 and 1988, the former award coming after a season in which Singletary anchored what is often considered the greatest defensive unit in professional football history, as the 1985 Bears allowed just 12.4 points per game in the regular season and won their three play-off games by a combined score of 91–10 en route to a Super Bowl title.

Following the end of his playing days, Singletary spent time as a motivational speaker before turning to coaching. In 2003 he became the linebackers coach for the Baltimore Ravens, and two years later he accepted the same position with the San Francisco 49ers. When head coach Mike Nolan was fired during the 49ers' 2008 campaign, Singletary was promoted to interim head coach. He led the team to a 5–4 record during the remainder of the season and was given the permanent head coaching position in 2009.

In 1998 Singletary was awarded his sport's highest honour when he was voted into the Pro Football Hall of Fame in his first year of eligibility.

ERIC DICKERSON

(b. Sept. 2, 1960, Sealy, Texas, U.S.)

Eric Dickerson is known as one of the leading running backs in NFL history.

Dickerson played his college football at Southern Methodist University in University Park, Texas, where he and Craig James formed a stellar backfield dubbed the "Pony Express" (after SMU's mustang mascot). Named an All-American in his senior season, Dickerson was drafted by the Los Angeles Rams with the second overall selection of the 1983 NFL draft. In his rookie year in the NFL, he led the league in rushing and earned All-Pro and Offensive Rookie of the Year honours. In 1984 Dickerson rushed for a league-record 2,105 yards. He again led the NFL in rushing in 1986 and 1988 — after being traded to the Indianapolis Colts in the middle of the 1987 season.

Later he played for the Los Angeles Raiders and the Atlanta Falcons. He retired soon after being traded to the Green Bay Packers in 1993, ending his 11-year NFL career after a damaged disk in his back made it too risky for him to play. He left the sport second only to Walter Payton as the leading rusher in NFL history up to that date, with 13,259 yards. Dickerson was inducted into the Pro Football Hall of Fame in 1999.

LAWRENCE TAYLOR

(b. Feb. 4, 1959, Williamsburg, Va., U.S.)

Lawrence Taylor redefined the linebacker position during his 13-year NFL career. As a member of the New York Giants, he won Super Bowl championships following the 1986 and 1990 seasons.

Taylor, who did not play organized football until the 11th grade, attended the University of North Carolina, where he initially played defensive lineman before being moved to outside linebacker. With a rare combination of size and speed, Taylor, 6 feet 3 inches (1.91 metres) tall and weighing 240 pounds (109 kg), excelled as a linebacker, and he was named All-American in 1980.

Taylor entered the NFL draft in 1981 and was the second overall pick, selected by the New York Giants. By the end of his first professional season, he had 9.5 quarterback

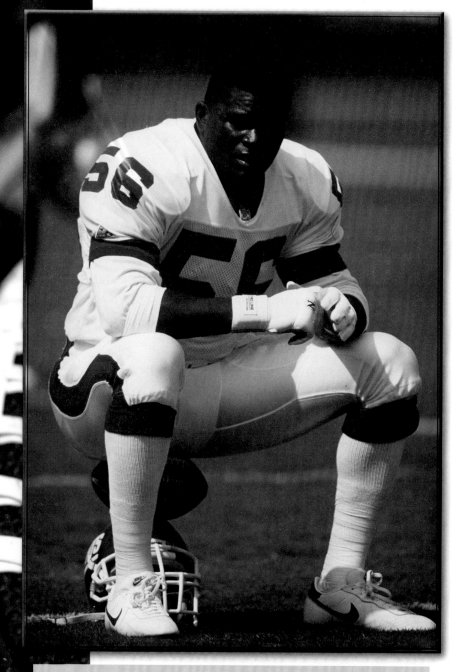

All-Pro linebacker Lawrence Taylor made headlines for his accomplishments on the field and his troubles off it. Ken Levine/Getty Images

sacks (an unofficial number, since the NFL did not keep statistics on sacks until the following season) and a reputation for making hard, vicious hits. He was named Rookie of the Year and Defensive Player of the Year, an honour that he received again the following season. In 1986 he led the league with 20.5 sacks, guided the Giants to victory over the Denver Broncos in Super Bowl XXI, and was named Most Valuable Player of the NFL—the second defensive player in league history to receive the honour. Taylor and the Giants won a second championship in January 1991, defeating the Buffalo Bills in Super Bowl XXV.

Often known simply as "L.T.," Taylor revolutionized the play of outside linebacker, traditionally a "read and react" position (the linebacker would watch the play develop, then move to stop it). Taylor was an attacking linebacker who possessed the strength and speed to make plays anywhere on the field. He was the most disruptive defensive player of his era. During his 13-year career, he was named All-Pro six times (1981–87) and made 10 Pro Bowl appearances (1981–90 seasons). He retired from professional football after the 1993 season with career totals of 132.5 sacks (not including sacks from his rookie year), 1,088 tackles, 33 forced fumbles, and 9 interceptions. He was enshrined in the Pro Football Hall of Fame in 1999.

Taylor's life off the field was troubled both during and after his football career. He struggled with a cocaine addiction, and in 1988 he was suspended by the NFL for failing a drug test. Between 1996 and 1998 he was arrested three times on drug charges. After completing a rehabilitation program in 1998, he pursued a career in acting. Taylor's *LT: Over the Edge* (2003; cowritten with Steve Serby) detailed his tumultuous past. In January 2011 he pleaded guilty to sexual misconduct and patronizing a prostitute—both misdemeanour charges—and was sentenced to six years of probation.

RONNIE LOTT

(b. May 8, 1959, Albuquerque, N.M., U.S.)

Ronnie Lott earned first-team All-Pro honours at all three defensive backfield positions during his standout 14-year NFL career. The preternaturally tough Lott is regarded as one of the hardest hitters in NFL history.

Ronald Mandel Lott attended the University of Southern California, where he was a consensus All-American safety in his senior year. He was selected by the San Francisco 49ers with the eighth selection of the 1981 NFL draft. Shifting from safety to cornerback, Lott started for the 49ers from the first game of his rookie year. He was named to both the Pro Bowl and All-Pro teams in his first year in the league as he helped the 49ers to their first Super Bowl title. Lott and San Francisco won a second Super Bowl in 1985, following a 15–1 regular season in which the 49ers' defense allowed the fewest points in the league. During the 1985 regular season Lott switched to free safety, where his aggressive tackling and nose for the ball were put to better use. At the end of that year he endured an injury that became a part of NFL lore and established his tough-guy reputation. After crushing a finger while making a tackle, he opted to have the top of the digit amputated rather than miss playing time in order to have reconstructive surgery.

In his five seasons as a full-time free safety in San Francisco (1986–90) he earned first-team All-Pro honours four times, and he anchored a 49ers defense that helped the team win two additional Super Bowls (1989–90). In 1991 he signed with the Los Angeles Raiders. In his first year with the franchise, after switching to strong safety, he led the league in interceptions and was named All-Pro at a third position. Lott joined the New York Jets in 1993 for two seasons before injuries forced him to leave the sport in 1995. At the time of his retirement, Lott had the fifth highest career interception total in league history. He became a successful businessman after his playing days ended, and he was inducted into the Pro Football Hall of Fame in 2000.

JOE MONTANA

(b. June 11, 1956, New Eagle, Pa., U.S.)

One of the greatest quarterbacks in the history of the NFL, Joe Montana led the San Francisco 49ers to four Super Bowl victories (1982, 1985, 1989, 1990) and was named the Super Bowl's Most Valuable Player (MVP) three times. He also ranks among football's all-time leaders in passing yards (40,551) and touchdown passes (273). Montana was known for his ability to calmly bring his team to victory from the brink of defeat during the final moments of the game, earning himself the nickname "Joe Cool."

Joseph Clifford Montana was raised in Monongahela, Pa., and excelled at baseball, basketball, and football in high school. He was offered a basketball scholarship to North Carolina State University in Raleigh, N.C., but instead went to the University of Notre Dame in South Bend, Ind., to play collegiate football. Montana began his junior year as the Fighting Irish's third-string quarterback but was elevated to starter after coming off the bench to lead Notre Dame to a comeback victory in the third game of the 1977 season. He finished that season by guiding once-beaten Notre Dame to the National Collegiate Athletic Association Division I-A national championship. After a successful senior year that ended with a Notre Dame victory in the Cotton Bowl, Montana was selected by the 49ers in the third round of the 1979 NFL draft.

Montana became the 49ers' starting quarterback midway through his second season in San Francisco. His field vision and keen decision making were ideal for head coach Bill Walsh's "West Coast offense," which relied on a series of short, accurate passes to move the ball downfield. Montana led the 49ers to their first Super Bowl victory in January 1982, earning game MVP honours in the process. His team's play-off run was highlighted by a game-winning touchdown pass from Montana to Dwight Clark with 51 seconds remaining in the NFC championship game, a play later known as "The Catch." The 49ers won a second Super Bowl title (and Montana a second Super Bowl MVP award) in 1985, defeating the Miami Dolphins.

The following spring the 49ers drafted wide receiver Jerry Rice, who teamed with Montana for six seasons to form one of the most prolific passing combinations in NFL history. In 1989 Montana led a dramatic late-game drive against the Cincinnati Bengals to win a third Super Bowl. Despite losing Walsh to retirement in the off-season, the 49ers repeated as champions the following year while posting the largest margin of victory in Super Bowl history (45 points), and Montana took home his third Super Bowl MVP trophy. In addition to his postseason accolades, Montana was named NFL MVP in 1989 and 1990.

An elbow injury forced Montana to miss all but one game over the course of the 1991 and 1992 seasons, and by the time he was ready to return to the field, future Hall of Famer Steve Young was entrenched as the 49ers starting quarterback. In 1993 Montana was traded to the Kansas City Chiefs. He earned a trip to the Pro Bowl in his first year in Kansas City (his eighth and final career selection) and led the Chiefs to play-off berths in his two seasons with the team. Montana retired in 1995, finishing his career with 31 fourth-quarter comeback victories and 10 play-off appearances in his 11 full seasons as a starting quarterback

Joe Montana is one of the most prolific and honoured quarterbacks in NFL history. Tony Duffy/Getty Images

in the NFL. He was elected to the Pro Football Hall of Fame in 2000.

JOHN ELWAY

(b. June 28, 1960, Port Angeles, Wash., U.S.)

John Elway led the Denver Broncos to two Super Bowl championships (1998, 1999).

Elway excelled at football and baseball in high school and was drafted by major league baseball's Kansas City Royals in 1979. However, he instead attended Stanford University (B.A., 1983) on a football scholarship, where he set several school and conference passing records. He was the number one draft pick of baseball's New York Yankees in 1981, and he played for a Yankees farm club over the following summer. In 1983 Elway was chosen by the Baltimore Colts as the first overall pick in the NFL draft, but he threatened to play baseball professionally if the struggling Colts did not trade him. The Colts complied, and Elway was dealt to the Denver Broncos, where he spent his entire 16-year career.

Elway impressed fans in the NFL with his throwing precision, cool leadership, and rushing ability. In his rookie year he led the Broncos to the franchise's fourth playoff appearance in its 24-year history. While Elway rarely led the league in individual statistical categories, he was noted for his consistent production and his ability to rally his team to victory in the late stages of games. The most famous of his comebacks came in the 1986 AFC championship game against the Cleveland Browns when he led the Broncos on a 98-yard drive to score the tying touchdown in the game's final seconds. The Broncos won the game in overtime to advance to the Super Bowl, and Elway's feat became known as "The Drive."

Elway's Broncos teams were unsuccessful in their first three Super Bowl appearances (1986, 1987, 1989), losing by an average margin of 32 points. In 1998, however, they finally broke through as Elway led another late-game drive to beat the Green Bay Packers in Super Bowl XXXII. The Broncos repeated as Super Bowl champions the following year, Elway's last. He retired with the NFL career records for most victories by a starting quarterback (148; which was broken by Brett Favre in 2007) and most fourth-quarter game-winning or game-tying drives (47). Elway was inducted into the Pro Football Hall of Fame in 2004.

BARRY SANDERS

(b. July 16, 1968, Wichita, Kan., U.S.)

In his 10 seasons with the Detroit Lions (1989–98), Barry Sanders led the NFL in rushing four times and was selected every year for the Pro Bowl. He was inducted into the Pro Football Hall of Fame in 2004.

In high school, Sanders's small stature of 5 feet 8 inches (1.73 metres) discouraged coaches from playing him at running back until the last five games of his senior year. The startling 1,417 yards that he gained, however, were enough to earn him a football scholarship to Oklahoma State University (OSU). Sanders became the starting halfback in 1988 and rushed for 2,628 yards—the best single-season rushing performance in the history of the National Collegiate Athletic Association—winning the Heisman Trophy that year as the nation's best college football player. When OSU was put on probation the next year, Sanders declared himself eligible for the professional draft and was selected by the Detroit Lions as the third overall pick.

Sanders set records for rushing more than 1,000 yards in 10 straight seasons, for rushing 1,500 yards or more in

5 different seasons (and the first to do so in 4 consecutive seasons), and for rushing more than 100 yards in 14 consecutive games. His most impressive season was 1997, when he became only the third back to rush for more than 2,000 yards; his 2,053 yards rushing and 305 yards in pass receptions, for a combined 2,358 yards, set a single-season record for running backs.

Like Jim Brown, Sanders left the game at or near his athletic peak. With 15,269 career rushing yards and 99 rushing touchdowns, Sanders was close to eclipsing Walter Payton's all-time records. Instead, Sanders was forced to return more than $5 million of his most recent signing bonus to the Detroit Lions after his early retirement.

DAN MARINO

(b. Sept. 15, 1961, Pittsburgh, Pa., U.S.)

Dan Marino was one of the most prolific passers in NFL history.

Daniel Constantine Marino, Jr., was a high school All-American in Pittsburgh, where he established himself as another of the great quarterbacks to hail from western Pennsylvania, alongside such luminaries as Johnny Unitas, Joe Montana, and Joe Namath. Unlike those quarterbacks, Marino stayed home to play at the University of Pittsburgh, earning All-American honours in his junior year. After a disappointing senior season by Marino's standards, his professional stock dropped, and he was chosen by the Miami Dolphins toward the end of the first round of the 1983 NFL draft.

Miami's investment paid immediate dividends. Marino stepped in as the team's starting quarterback six games into his rookie year. He then led the Dolphins to a play-off berth and was named to the Pro Bowl. In 1984 he became the first quarterback to pass for more than 5,000 yards in a single season (5,084) and the first to complete over 40 touchdown passes (48) in a season (his touchdown record has since been broken). Marino was named the NFL's Most Valuable Player, and at the end of that season he made the only Super Bowl appearance of his career; the Dolphins lost that game to Montana and the San Francisco 49ers.

Over the course of his career, he led the NFL in passing yards on four more occasions (1985, 1986, 1988, 1992) and in touchdown passes an additional two times (1985, 1986). Marino and the Dolphins appeared in the conference championship game in 1985 and 1992, but Miami advanced no further than that point in the postseason during his 17-year career. Although his teams were not as successful as those of other elite quarterbacks, Marino was nevertheless one of the most dominant players at his position: by the end of his final season (1999), he had set all-time records for passes completed (4,453 in 7,452 attempts), yards passing (55,416), touchdown passes (385), and a number of other categories. (Marino's most prominent career marks were later broken by Brett Favre.)

He was a prominent pitchman for a number of products both before and after his retirement. Upon leaving the sport, he became a football commentator on television. A three-time All-Pro selection and nine-time Pro Bowl honoree, Marino was inducted into the Pro Football Hall of Fame in 2005.

JOHN MADDEN

(b. April 10, 1936, Austin, Minn., U.S.)

Football coach and television commentator John Madden was one of the best-known personalities in NFL history. In addition to his accomplishments in the NFL, Madden

John Madden, 2006. Madden played football in college and coached in the NFL, but he is arguably better known as a commentator and pitchman.
Jonathan Daniel/Getty Images

lent his name to a series of video games, *Madden NFL*, that became a cultural sensation.

Madden was raised in Daly City, Calif., where he was a standout high school football player. He played on both the offensive and the defensive line at California Polytechnic State University (at San Luis Obispo) and was drafted by the Philadelphia Eagles in 1958. However, a knee injury he suffered during his first training camp prevented him from launching a playing career in the NFL. He coached at Hancock Junior College in Santa Maria, Calif., from 1960 to 1963, and was the defensive coordinator at San Diego State University from 1964 to 1966. In 1967 Madden was hired by Al Davis as the Oakland Raiders' linebackers coach. Madden was promoted to head coach in February 1969 at age 32.

In Madden's first season at the helm, the Raiders posted a 12–1–1 record and lost to the Kansas City Chiefs in the AFL championship game. After the 1970 AFL-NFL merger, the Raiders appeared in four AFC championship games over the course of six seasons but lost on each occasion. Just as criticism that Madden could not win the big game reached its peak, he led the Raiders to a one-loss season in 1976, which the team followed with victories over the rival Pittsburgh Steelers in the AFC championship game and over the Minnesota Vikings in Super Bowl XI. Madden stepped away from the Raiders following the 1978 season having never had a losing record in his 10 seasons as head coach. He was inducted into the Pro Football Hall of Fame in 2006.

Though his coaching success had brought him fame, it was in his next career—as a football analyst for television—that Madden became an icon inextricably linked to the NFL. His first position as a colour commentator came in 1979 at CBS. In 1981 he was paired with play-by-play announcer Pat Summerall, with whom Madden would form a 21-year partnership that made the pair arguably the most famous sports broadcasting duo of all time; the two moved to the Fox Broadcasting Company in 1994. Madden's idiosyncratic commentary—which included a willingness to explicate the most complicated or obscure details of a football game; his frequent use of, and subsequent popularization of, the Telestrator, a device that allows its user to draw on top of an image from a broadcast; and his penchant for sudden outbursts (most notably "Boom!") while analyzing a play—endeared him to many viewers (while alienating some others) and helped Madden garner a record 16 Emmy Awards for outstanding sports analyst/personality. He was famous for a fear of flying that resulted in his traveling to all of his broadcast locations in a customized bus nicknamed the "Madden Cruiser," which became something of a minor NFL icon itself. Madden was also known for selecting an annual "All-Madden" team made up of players he believed were the toughest and smartest in the game. After working for all four of the major American broadcasting networks over the course of his career, he retired in 2009.

Madden's outsized personality made him an ideal pitchman for a vast number of products, from beer to hardware stores. In 1989 he gave his name to the computer game *John Madden Football*. The subsequent *Madden NFL* series expanded onto multiple gaming consoles and grew into the most popular sports title on the market by the early 2000s, with the annual release of an increasingly detailed and realistic new edition becoming a highly anticipated event among both football fans and NFL players. As a result of its massive popularity, the video game helped to increase football's global audience and, in turn, Madden's fame.

Madden authored (with cowriter Dave Anderson) a number of best-selling books, including *Hey, Wait a Minute, I Wrote a Book* (1984), *One Size Doesn't Fit All* (1988), and *All Madden: Hey, I'm Talking Pro Football!* (1996).

REGGIE WHITE

(b. Dec. 19, 1961, Chattanooga, Tenn., U.S.—d. Dec. 26, 2004,
Huntersville, N.C.)

Reggie White was one of the most dominant defensive
linemen in the history of the sport. In his 15-year NFL
career, he was selected to the Pro Bowl 13 consecutive
times, and, at the time of his retirement in 2000, he was
the NFL's all-time career leader in sacks with 198.

Reginald Howard White played football at the
University of Tennessee, where he was an All-American
his senior year. The 6-foot 5-inch (1.96-metre), 300-pound
(136-kg) defensive lineman began his professional career
in 1984 playing for the United States Football League
(USFL) Memphis Showboats, where he had 11 sacks and
was named to the all-rookie team. After two seasons in
the USFL, he was acquired in the NFL supplemental draft
by the Philadelphia Eagles, for which he played from 1985
to 1992. In 1987 he recorded 21 sacks and was the league's
Defensive Player of the Year.

In 1993 the NFL instituted full free agency for the first
time, and White became the most sought-after player on
the market. He signed with the Green Bay Packers after a
long courtship process. White's dominant play continued
with his new team, and he helped shape Green Bay into
one of the premier defensive teams in the NFL. In 1997 the
Packers made it to their first Super Bowl in 29 years, where
they defeated the New England Patriots. White won his
second Defensive Player of the Year award in 1998 after
posting 16 sacks during the regular season, and he abruptly
retired after Green Bay's opening-round play-off loss in the
following postseason. After one year away from the sport,
he signed with the Carolina Panthers, where he recorded a
career-low 5.5 sacks in his one season with the team.

White was an ordained Baptist minister, which was the source of his nickname, the "Minister of Defense." *Reggie White in the Trenches: The Autobiography* appeared in 1996. White was posthumously inducted into the Pro Football Hall of Fame in 2006.

BRUCE SMITH

(b. June 18, 1963, Norfolk, Va., U.S.)

Defensive end Bruce Smith holds the NFL career record for quarterback sacks (200).

Smith played college football at Virginia Tech, where he was a consensus All-American and won the Outland Trophy as the best lineman in the country during his senior season. He was selected by the Buffalo Bills with the first overall pick of the 1985 NFL draft. Smith totaled 15 sacks in his second season, the first of 13 seasons in which he recorded at least 10 sacks. His rare combination of size (6 feet 4 inches [1.93 metres], 262 pounds [119 kg]) and quickness promptly made him one of the most difficult defensive players in the league to block: Smith was often too fast for offensive tackles and too powerful for tight ends and running backs.

In 1990 he had 19 sacks and a remarkable—for his position—101 tackles, which earned him the NFL Defensive Player of the Year award. That postseason he helped the Bills win the conference championship and advance to the Super Bowl. It was the first of four consecutive Super Bowl berths for Smith and the Bills, but the team lost the game each time. Smith was named the league's Defensive Player of the Year for a second time in 1996 after amassing 13.5 sacks.

After 15 seasons with the Bills in which he was named first-team All-Pro eight times and earned 11 Pro Bowl berths, he signed with the Washington Redskins in 2000. Smith spent four mostly nondescript years in Washington,

Bruce Smith recorded 10 or more quarterback sacks in 12 of his 15 seasons with the Buffalo Bills. As of 2011, he held the record for most career sacks (200). Rick Stewart/Getty Images

the highlight of which came in 2003, when he broke Reggie White's career sack record of 198. He then retired after the 2003 season. Smith was inducted into the Pro Football Hall of Fame in 2009, his first year of eligibility for that honour.

JERRY RICE

(b. Oct. 13, 1962, Starkville, Miss., U.S.)

Jerry Rice is considered by most observers to be the greatest wide receiver in the history of the NFL. Playing primarily for the San Francisco 49ers, he set a host of NFL records, including those for career touchdowns (208), receptions (1,549), and reception yardage (22,895).

The son of a brick mason, Rice was celebrated for having developed strong, reliable hands by catching bricks that his brothers threw to him while working for their father. He attended Mississippi Valley State University in Itta Bena on a football scholarship. There he earned All-America honours and set 18 records in Division I-AA of the National Collegiate Athletic Association, including most catches in a single game (24).

Rice was drafted by the San Francisco 49ers in the first round of the 1985 NFL draft. He initially struggled to hold on to the ball as he concentrated on the intricate pass patterns of the San Francisco offense, but in his second season he caught 86 passes and led the league in reception yardage (1,570) and touchdown receptions (15). Rice thrived in San Francisco head coach Bill Walsh's "West Coast offense," which relied on a large number of short, quick passes by the quarterback and precise route running by the receivers. He set a single-season record for touchdown receptions (22) in 1987, even though a players' strike limited the season to 12 games, and was named NFL Player of the Year. Standing 6 feet 2 inches (1.9 metres) tall, Rice was larger than the typical NFL wide receiver, and he used his size and strength to overmatch defenders. He was also an exceptional runner after making a catch.

Rice played on three Super Bowl championship teams with the 49ers (1988, 1989, and 1994 seasons), and he, along with quarterback Joe Montana and defensive back Ronnie Lott, became virtually synonymous with the team. He was named the Most Valuable Player of Super Bowl XXIII (1988 season), and he set numerous Super Bowl records. Rice was named to the annual Pro Bowl from 1986 through 1998. In a controversial move to develop younger players, the 49ers traded Rice to the Oakland Raiders before the 2001 season. The following season he became the first player to register more than 200 career touchdowns as he helped the Raiders reach Super Bowl XXXVII, where they were defeated by the Tampa Bay Buccaneers. In 2003 he made his 13th Pro Bowl appearance. Midway through the 2004 season, Rice was traded to the Seattle Seahawks, but he was released by the team at the end of the season. After an unsuccessful attempt to become a starting receiver for the Denver Broncos the following year, he signed a ceremonial one-day contract with San Francisco and retired as a 49er. Rice was inducted into the Pro Football Hall of Fame in 2010.

EMMITT SMITH

(b. May 15, 1969, Pensacola, Fla., U.S.)

In 2002 Emmitt Smith became the all-time leading rusher in NFL history. He retired after the 2004 season with 18,355 yards rushing, and also holds the record for most rushing touchdowns in a career, with 164.

Smith excelled early in football, starring in youth leagues and, by the time he finished high school, earning national Player of the Year honours from *Parade* magazine, among other publications. He played collegiate football at the

University of Florida (in Gainesville), where he amassed 58 school records before leaving the school after his junior year.

Selected in the first round of the 1990 NFL draft by the Dallas Cowboys, Smith soon established himself as one of the league's premier running backs. He was named NFL Offensive Rookie of the Year in 1990 and the following season ran for 1,563 yards to capture the first of his four NFL rushing titles (the other three came in 1992–93, 1995). With quarterback Troy Aikman and wide receiver Michael Irvin, Smith was part of a formidable Dallas offense that helped the Cowboys win consecutive Super Bowls over the Buffalo Bills in 1993 and 1994. He rushed for 1,486 yards during the 1993 regular season—averaging a tremendous 5.3 yards per carry—and was named the NFL's Most Valuable Player. Smith won a third Super Bowl championship in 1996. His rushing totals began to fall off in the late 1990s, and the Cowboys released him after the 2002 season. Smith then signed with the Arizona Cardinals, finishing his career with two relatively nondescript seasons in Arizona.

Though Smith was relatively small—he stood only 5 feet 9 inches (1.75 metres) tall and weighed 212 pounds (96 kg)—and lacked great speed, he thrived in the NFL by relying on his strength, determination, and superb conditioning. He ultimately proved to be one of the NFL's most durable players at any position; between 1990 and 2002 he failed to start in only two games. An eight-time Pro Bowl selection over the course of his career, he was inducted into the Pro Football Hall of Fame in 2010.

DEION SANDERS

(b. Aug. 9, 1967, Fort Myers, Fla., U.S.)

Football and baseball player Deion Sanders is the only person to have played in both a Super Bowl and a World

Series. Known for his flashy personality and outspokenness, which garnered him the nicknames "Prime Time" and "Neon Deion," Sanders was a middling professional baseball player but is widely considered the best man-to-man cover cornerback in NFL history.

Sanders was a multisport star in high school and earned a scholarship to Florida State University, where he was a member of the school's football, baseball, and track teams. He first brought his brash attitude to national attention as a two-time All-American in football. Sanders quickly became a sports media favourite, and his tremendous on-field achievements were sometimes overshadowed by his braggadocio, his penchant for gaudy jewelry, and his self-promotion, which included his tuxedo-attired arrival in a white stretch limousine at a 1988 game against the rival University of Florida. NFL teams were not put off by his cocky persona, however, and Sanders was selected by the Atlanta Falcons with the fifth selection of the 1989 NFL draft.

Sanders played primarily in the New York Yankees' minor league system in 1989 but was called up for 14 games in the majors that summer. After posting a .158 batting average in 57 games with the Yankees in 1990, he was released and then signed by the Atlanta Braves. The speedy outfielder had the best season of his baseball career in 1992, batting .304 with a league-leading 14 triples as he helped the Braves reach the World Series (a six-game loss to the Toronto Blue Jays). He was traded to the Cincinnati Reds during the 1994 season and then to the San Francisco Giants during the 1995 season. After not playing in 1996, Sanders had one-year stints with the Reds in 1997 and 2001 before retiring from baseball.

In his much more successful professional football career, Sanders made an immediate impact. He intercepted five passes in his rookie season, was a full-time starter in his second, and was named to his first of eight Pro Bowls in his third. He signed a one-year contract with the San Francisco 49ers for the 1994 season, during which he was named NFL Defensive Player of the Year after making six interceptions (returning three for touchdowns) and helped the team to a decisive victory in Super Bowl XXIX. In 1995–96 he won another Super Bowl title in his first season with the Dallas Cowboys, with whom he played for four more seasons before moving to the Washington Redskins for the 2000 season. Sanders then retired for three years only to return for a two-season stint with the Baltimore Ravens before permanently leaving the sport in 2006.

That his interception totals were lower than those of most other elite cornerbacks is attributable to the fact that opposing teams often simply avoided throwing the ball in his vicinity. On the other hand, noting that Sanders's tackling and run-stopping abilities were often lacking, some have said that he was not a complete cornerback. Sanders's speed and elusiveness made him one of the best kickoff and punt returners of all time, as well as an effective occasional receiving option on offense, with 60 career receptions (three for touchdowns) to his credit. The 19 non-offensive touchdowns (combining kickoff, punt, interception, and fumble returns) he scored over the course of his career were an NFL record at the time of his retirement.

After his playing days ended, Sanders spent time as a television football analyst and starred in a short-lived reality television series. His eventual alienation from his freewheeling lifestyle was documented in *Power, Money & Sex: How Success Almost Ruined My Life* (1998; cowritten with Jim Nelson Black). Sanders was inducted into the Pro Football Hall of Fame in 2011.

CHAPTER 7
OTHER PRO AND COLLEGE FOOTBALL GREATS

While collegiate football has its own Hall of Fame, it is not as prestigious as the Pro Football Hall of Fame in Canton. Nevertheless, there are a number of individuals who had great success at the collegiate level and made a lasting impact on the history of the sport. This chapter highlights those college greats as well as NFL stars who have not yet been inducted into the Pro Football Hall of Fame. (The following biographies are arranged alphabetically.)

BOBBY BOWDEN

(b. Nov. 8, 1929, Birmingham, Ala., U.S.)

Bobby Bowden is one of the winningest coaches in National Collegiate Athletic Association (NCAA) history.

Robert Cleckler Bowden played quarterback at the University of Alabama as a freshman but, in accordance with university policy at the time, was forced to give up his scholarship after marrying his high school sweetheart. He then transferred to Howard College (now Samford University) in his hometown, Birmingham, Ala. After graduating from Howard in 1953, Bowden was an assistant football coach there for two years before becoming the athletic director and head coach at South Georgia

College (1956–58), a two-year institution. He returned to Howard in 1959 as head coach, but he left the school in 1962 to become an assistant coach at the highest level of collegiate football (the University Division, now called the Football Bowl Subdivision), first as the wide receivers coach at Florida State University (1963–65) and then as the offensive coordinator at West Virginia University (1966–69). He was promoted to head coach at West Virginia in 1970. Bowden had a 42–26 record at West Virginia and guided the Mountaineers to two bowl appearances before taking the head coaching position at Florida State in 1976.

It was at Florida State that Bowden became a coaching icon. His 5–6 record in 1976 was the only losing record he posted as the team's head coach. In 1982 Florida State went 9–3 and received an invitation to the Gator Bowl, which began a streak of 28 consecutive bowl appearances for the Seminoles under Bowden. In 1993 Florida State went 12–1 and captured its first national championship. Bowden led Florida State to a second national championship in 1999, as the undefeated Seminoles became the first team in college football history to be voted number one in the Associated Press (AP) poll in every week of the season. Between 1987 and 2000 he guided the Seminoles to an extraordinary 14 consecutive top-five finishes in the AP poll.

In the first decade of the 21st century, Bowden and Pennsylvania State University's Joe Paterno were in a back-and-forth race for the all-time record for "major college" coaching victories in a career. Some observers questioned the validity of Bowden's wins at Howard College, which included victories over junior colleges and a freshman team. However, the controversy became moot in 2010 — just weeks after Bowden's retirement—when the NCAA stripped Florida State of 12 wins from the 2006 and 2007 seasons after the football program was found guilty of widespread academic fraud.

Bowden officially amassed 377 wins (as well as 129 losses and 4 ties) in his 44-year non-junior-college coaching career. In addition, he led Florida State to 12 Atlantic Coast Conference titles in the 18 seasons the formerly independent Seminoles played in the conference during his tenure. He was inducted into the College Football Hall of Fame in 2006.

TOM BRADY

(b. Aug. 3, 1977, San Mateo, Calif., U.S.)

Quarterback Tom Brady led the New England Patriots to three Super Bowl victories (2002, 2004, 2005) and was twice named the game's Most Valuable Player (MVP; 2002, 2004).

While growing up, Thomas Edward Patrick Brady, Jr., often attended San Francisco 49ers games to watch the legendary quarterback Joe Montana—Brady's idol and the man to whom he would eventually be compared—play during the 1980s. In high school Brady excelled in both football and baseball. He entered the major league baseball draft in 1995 and was picked by the Montreal Expos, but he decided instead to attend the University of Michigan and play football. Brady, who did not start until his junior year, led Michigan to victory in the 1999 Orange Bowl and gained a reputation as a determined and intelligent player but one who lacked any exceptional physical skills. In 2000 he was chosen in the sixth round of the NFL draft by New England, and he worked diligently during his first season to bulk up physically and improve his strength and technique.

In the second game of the 2001 season, the Patriots' starting quarterback, Drew Bledsoe, was injured, and

Quarterback Tom Brady hoisting the Lombardi Trophy after the New England Patriots won the Super Bowl in 2004. Elsa/Getty Images

Brady was chosen to fill the position. His play was not spectacular, but he was consistent, making simple plays and minimizing mistakes. With Brady as their starting quarterback, the Patriots went on to post an 11–3 record in the regular season and to upset the St. Louis Rams in Super Bowl XXXVI; Brady was named the Super Bowl MVP. The Patriots became one of the NFL's elite teams, posting an incredible 40–12 record during Brady's first three seasons. In 2004 the team returned to the Super Bowl, defeating the Carolina Panthers and earning Brady another Super Bowl MVP award. The momentum carried through to the next season, as the Patriots extended their consecutive win streak to 21, breaking the record of 18 set by the Miami Dolphins in 1972–73. Brady and the Patriots capped off the season with their third Super Bowl in four years, this time against the Philadelphia Eagles.

In the 2007 season Brady threw a record 50 touchdown passes, and he led New England to the first 16–0 regular season in NFL history. However, the Patriots lost to the underdog New York Giants in Super Bowl XLII. In the first game of the 2008 NFL schedule, Brady suffered a severe knee injury that required season-ending surgery. He returned to form the next season, earning his fifth career Pro Bowl selection after guiding the Patriots to another play-off berth. While not the strongest or the quickest quarterback in the NFL, Brady established himself among the game's greats for his tenacity, his intelligent playmaking abilities, and the remarkable leadership he provided under pressure.

Brady appeared as himself in various television shows, including *Entourage*, and provided his voice in the animated series *Family Guy* and *The Simpsons*. In 2009 he married fashion model Gisele Bündchen.

DERRICK BROOKS

(b. April 18, 1973, Pensacola, Fla., U.S.)

In his 14-year career with the Tampa Bay Buccaneers, Derrick Brooks established himself as one of the greatest linebackers in the history of the sport.

Brooks was a standout safety in high school and was recruited to play that position at Florida State University. The team's coaching staff switched him to outside linebacker late in his freshman year, and, though undersized (6 feet [1.83 metres], 210 pounds [95 kg]) for the position, Brooks excelled, earning consensus All-American honours as a junior and senior. He was selected by the Buccaneers in the first round of the 1995 NFL draft.

When Brooks joined the team, the Buccaneers were a long-woeful franchise, having lost 10 or more games for 12 consecutive seasons between 1983 and 1994. Brooks was the key piece of a turnaround in Tampa Bay, as the Bucs defense quickly became one of the most dominant units in the league, finishing in the top 10 in fewest yards allowed in nine straight seasons from 1997. He excelled in the team's signature defensive alignment—the "Tampa 2"—which made great use of his excellent instincts and sure tackling ability. Brooks helped the team to seven play-off appearances in his 14 years with Tampa Bay, one of which ended in the franchise's first Super Bowl victory (2003). Over the course of his professional career, he added 25 pounds [11 kg] of muscle but maintained the exceptional speed he had as a young defensive back, which helped him amass 25 career interceptions.

Brooks was the 2002 NFL Defensive Player of the Year, a five-time first-team All-Pro selection, and was named to 11 career Pro Bowls. He was released by the Buccaneers in 2009 and officially retired in 2010 after failing to sign with another team.

BEAR BRYANT

(b. Sept. 11, 1913, Kingsland, Ark., U.S.—d. Jan. 26, 1983, Tuscaloosa, Ala.)

Bear Bryant was a college football coach who set a record for more games won than any other collegiate coach.

Paul William Bryant played tackle and was all-state at Fordyce (Ark.) High School; he went on to the University of Alabama, Tuscaloosa (1932–36; B.S., 1936), where he played blocking end. During his collegiate career the team won 23 games, lost 3, and tied 2. He played on the team that beat Stanford University in the Rose Bowl game (1935).

Bryant was an assistant coach at Alabama (1936–40) and at Vanderbilt University in Nashville (1940–41). After serving in the Navy during World War II, he began his career as a head coach in 1945 at the University of Maryland, College Park. Bryant resigned after the president reinstated an athlete Bryant had dismissed for breaking training rules. At the University of Kentucky, Lexington (1946–53), his team won 60 games, lost 23, and tied 5; won the school's first Southeastern Conference championship; and won three of four bowl games. Bryant left Kentucky after losing a battle of wills with Adolph Rupp as to whether basketball or football should be the dominant sport.

In 1954, Bryant's first year as a coach at Texas Agricultural and Mechanical University, College Station, the team lost 9 of 10 games. In the next three seasons, however, they lost only four games and won one Southwest Conference championship.

In 1958 Bryant returned to Alabama, where he spent the rest of his coaching career. In 1971 he recruited the first black player on the Alabama team, and he was credited with helping to stimulate the integration of college football at mostly white Southern universities. Alabama won six national championships (1961, 1964–65, 1973, 1978–79), and Bryant was named national coach of the year three times. Alabama played in 24 straight bowl games, including the 1982 Liberty Bowl, played on December 29, which was Bryant's last game and final victory. In all, Bryant, who prowled the sidelines in his trademark houndstooth fedora, took Alabama to 28 bowl games. Bryant's teams at Alabama averaged 9.28 victories a year, an average unequalled by any other college coach. Bryant's career coaching record of 323 regular season wins, 85 losses, and 17 ties broke the long-standing record of Amos Alonzo Stagg for most games won by a college coach. The record of 323 wins stood until it was broken by Eddie Robinson in 1985. Notable among Bryant's players were the future professional quarterbacks George Blanda, Joe Namath, and Ken Stabler.

ERNIE DAVIS

(b. Dec. 14, 1939, New Salem, Pa., U.S.—d. May 18, 1963, Cleveland, Ohio)

Ernie Davis was the first African American to win the Heisman Trophy.

As a student at Elmira (N.Y.) Free Academy, Ernest R. Davis was a high school All-American in football and basketball. Widely recruited to play running back in collegiate football, he chose to attend Syracuse University, in part because it was the school of his idol, Jim Brown. Davis wore Brown's number 44 at Syracuse, and in his sophomore year there he led the Orangemen to an undefeated season and a national championship. Syracuse clinched the national title with a 23–14 victory over the University of Texas in the 1960 Cotton Bowl. The game was highlighted by Davis's two touchdowns, which earned him Cotton Bowl Most Valuable Player honours. He was named an All-American in both his junior and senior seasons at Syracuse, and in

1961 he was awarded the Heisman Trophy as the most outstanding player in American college football—the first African American so honoured.

Davis was selected with the first overall pick of the 1962 NFL draft by the Washington Redskins, who then traded him to the Cleveland Browns, whose owner Art Modell planned to pair Davis with Jim Brown in the team's backfield. Davis never played a game for the Browns, however, as he was diagnosed with leukemia before the College All-Star Game in July 1962. He underwent a variety of treatments in an attempt to return to football, but they were all unsuccessful; he died in a Cleveland hospital in 1963. Davis, who was nicknamed the "Elmira Express," was posthumously inducted into the College Football Hall of Fame in 1979.

BRETT FAVRE

(b. Oct. 10, 1969, Gulfport, Miss., U.S.),

Brett Favre broke all the major NFL career passing records, primarily as quarterback of the Green Bay Packers.

Favre grew up in Kiln, Miss., and attended the University of Southern Mississippi, where he became the football team's starting quarterback while a freshman. He was drafted by the NFL's Atlanta Falcons in 1991 but was traded to Green Bay the following year after falling out of favour with Atlanta's coaching staff. Originally a backup quarterback, he started for an injured teammate in the third game of the 1992 season and never relinquished the position. In 1993 Favre led the Packers to their first playoff appearance in 10 years, and he established himself as one of the premier quarterbacks in the NFL. Known for his agility, competitiveness, and field presence, he was named the league's Most Valuable Player (MVP) a record three consecutive times (1995, 1996, 1997) and led the league in touchdown passes in each MVP year.

At the end of the 1996 season, Favre led the Packers to victory over the New England Patriots in Super Bowl XXXI. He returned to the Super Bowl the following year, but the Packers lost to John Elway's Denver Broncos in the waning minutes of the game. The Packers were less successful in the years following their two Super Bowl runs, but Favre continued to be productive. He led the league in pass completions in 1998 and 2005, and he had the most passing yards and touchdown passes in 1998 and 2003, respectively. He finished in the top 10 in completions, passing yards, and touchdown passes in every season between 1992 and 2007. In addition to these single-season accomplishments, Favre reached unprecedented individual statistical milestones over the course of his career. In the 2007 season he broke Elway's record of 148 career wins as a starting quarterback and Dan Marino's all-time records of 420 touchdown passes and 61,371 passing yards, as well as George Blanda's career interception record of 277. Favre announced his retirement from professional football at the end of the 2007 NFL season.

In July 2008 Favre let it be known that he wanted to return to the NFL, and he was reinstated by the league the following month. However, his strained relationship with Packers management—as well as the team's commitment to a new starting quarterback—led the Packers to trade him to the New York Jets before the start of the 2008 NFL season. While he was named to his 10th career Pro Bowl in 2008, Favre's one season with the Jets was nevertheless a disappointment. Not only did he lead the league in interceptions and finish the year ranked 21st in passer rating, but, after an 8–3 start, the Jets won a total of only nine games and missed the play-offs. Citing diminished playing skills and an injured biceps tendon, Favre retired once more in February 2009. His previous indecision led many to speculate that he would end his second retirement as the NFL season neared, and, just weeks after publicly stating that he would not be returning, in August 2009 Favre signed to play with the Minnesota Vikings.

Favre had one of his best seasons in 2009: he set career highs in completion percentage and passer rating and threw only seven interceptions. He guided the Vikings to a 12–4 record and a berth in the NFC championship game. However, his remarkable season ended on a sour note, as he threw a last-minute interception with the Vikings in range of a game-winning field goal attempt, which allowed the New Orleans Saints to win the NFC championship in overtime.

DOUG FLUTIE

(b. Oct. 23, 1962, Manchester, Md., U.S.)

After winning the Heisman Trophy in 1984 as the best player in college football, Doug Flutie had a 21-year professional football career in the United States and Canada.

Douglas Richard Flutie was a standout player at Natick (Mass.) High School, but Boston College was the only NCAA Division I-A (now the Football Bowl Subdivision) school to offer him a scholarship. He became that school's starting quarterback during his freshman season, and in his sophomore year he guided it to its first postseason bowl appearance in 40 years. His senior season was highlighted by an iconic 48-yard "Hail Mary" touchdown pass that Flutie threw as time was running out to beat the University of Miami in a key late-season game. His 3,454 passing yards and 27 touchdowns that year earned him All-America honours and the first Heisman Trophy in Boston College history. By the end of his collegiate career, Flutie had set all-time NCAA Division I-A records (since broken) for passing yards and total yards of offense.

Aware that his 5-foot 9-inch (1.75-metre) height would prevent him from being considered a suitable candidate to play in the NFL, Flutie signed a contract with the New Jersey Generals of the upstart United States Football League (USFL) instead. The USFL folded after his first season, and his NFL rights (he had been selected as an 11th-round draft pick by the Los Angeles Rams in 1985 after signing with the Generals) were traded to the Chicago Bears. In 1986 he made his NFL debut with the Bears but played in only five games before being traded to the New England Patriots the following year. After the 1989 season he was released by the Patriots, and in 1990 he signed with the British Columbia Lions of the Canadian Football League (CFL). The CFL, with its wider field and strong emphasis on passing, was a perfect fit for Flutie and his freewheeling scrambling style of play. During an eight-year CFL career, he was named the league's Most Outstanding Player an unprecedented six times, and three of the teams for which he played won the Grey Cup.

With more than 40,000 yards, 270 passing touchdowns, and 70 rushing touchdowns to his credit in the CFL, Flutie was signed by the NFL's Buffalo Bills to serve as a backup quarterback at the start of the 1998 season. When the starter went down with a rib injury five games into the season, Flutie seized his chance and threw for 2,711 yards and 20 touchdowns while leading the Bills to a 7–3 record in 10 starts. The Bills advanced to the play-offs, and Flutie was named to the Pro Bowl. He remained the team's starting quarterback in 1999 — when he again guided the Bills to the postseason — but was relegated to backup duty in 2000. In 2001 Flutie left the Bills and signed with the San Diego Chargers. After seeing the Chargers post a 5–11 record in his first season with the team, Flutie was again demoted to backup status. He rejoined New England in 2005 but retired the following year. Flutie subsequently served as a television college football analyst. In 2007 he was inducted into the College Football Hall of Fame.

WOODY HAYES

(b. Feb. 14, 1913, Clifton, Ohio, U.S.—d. March 12, 1987, Upper Arlington, Ohio)

Acclaimed college football coach Woody Hayes developed 58 All-American players over the course of his career, and his Ohio State University teams (1951–78) won 3 national championships (1954, 1957, and 1968) and 13 Big Ten championships and played in 8 Rose Bowl games (winning 4).

Wayne Woodrow Hayes graduated in 1935 from Denison University in Ohio and then taught and coached football in Ohio high schools (1936–40). In World War II he served in the U.S. Navy (1941–46). After the war he coached at Denison (1946–48) and at Miami University (Oxford, Ohio; 1949–50).

In 1951 he became head coach at Ohio State. There he became known as a conservative coach and a stern taskmaster; during games he was aggressive and defiant, berating officials and destroying sideline yard markers in his wrath. His iron-fisted style was accepted, even celebrated, in the 1950s and '60s, but as times changed, Hayes did not. He was discharged as coach in 1978 after a nationally televised game during which he struck a Clemson University player who had intercepted an Ohio State pass. His career coaching record was 238 games won, 72 lost, and 10 tied, and he was elected to the College Football Hall of Fame in 1983.

RAY LEWIS

(b. May 15, 1975, Bartow, Fla., U.S.)

Ray Lewis is considered to be one of the greatest linebackers in NFL history.

After starring in several sports in high school, Lewis enrolled at the University of Miami in Florida, where he became a middle linebacker and was named to the Freshman All-America team. In his junior year—his last at the university—Lewis finished the season with a team-high 160 tackles and earned All-America honours. He was selected by the Baltimore Ravens with the 26th overall selection of the 1996 NFL draft. In 1997 he led the league in tackles and played in his first Pro Bowl.

During the off-season in 2000, Lewis encountered legal difficulties. On January 31 he and several friends attended a post–Super Bowl party at a nightclub in Atlanta, and, as the party was breaking up, a fight erupted outside the club. When it was over, two men had been stabbed to death, and Lewis and two companions were eventually charged with the murders. During a four-week trial in the spring of 2000, the charge against Lewis was dropped (he pleaded guilty to one count of obstruction of justice in exchange for testifying against his codefendants), but his reputation was nevertheless tarnished, and many wondered if his play would be adversely affected. However, the following autumn he led a Baltimore defense that finished the regular season as the highest ranked in the league and gained a reputation as one of the best players in NFL history. Lewis was named the NFL's Defensive Player of the Year for his efforts, and the Ravens finished the year by beginning an unexpected postseason run that saw them earn the franchise's first Super Bowl berth in January 2001. Lewis led his team to a convincing 34–7 victory over

Ray Lewis was named game MVP in the Baltimore Ravens' Super Bowl win over the New York Giants in 2001. Jim Rogash/Getty Images

the New York Giants, and he was named the game's Most Valuable Player.

In 2001 Lewis was selected to his fifth consecutive Pro Bowl and was named All-Pro for a third straight year, but a separated shoulder in 2002 limited him to just five games. He returned the next season and won his second Defensive Player of the Year award after again leading the NFL in tackles. After suffering a serious hamstring injury in 2005, Lewis headed his second top-ranked defense in 2006, and in 2009 he was named All-Pro for a seventh time.

PEYTON MANNING

(b. March 24, 1976, New Orleans, La., U.S.)

One of the NFL's most celebrated quarterbacks, Peyton Manning led the Indianapolis Colts to a Super Bowl victory in 2007.

Manning was immersed in football from a very young age. His father, Archie Manning, was a star quarterback with the New Orleans Saints. (Younger brother Eli also became an NFL quarterback, and he led the New York Giants to a victory in Super Bowl XLII.) A highly regarded high school player, Peyton Manning received a national Player of the Year award in his senior season. He attended the University of Tennessee, where he was the starting quarterback for four years. Manning earned the Sullivan Award as the country's top amateur athlete in 1996, was selected a first-team All-American in 1997, and finished his collegiate career in 1998 as Tennessee's career passing leader.

Manning was selected with the first overall pick of the 1998 NFL draft by the Indianapolis Colts. In 1999 he helped the Colts win the franchise's first division title since 1987. The following season Manning threw for 4,413 yards and

Peyton Manning comes from a family of gifted quarterbacks. Jonathan Daniel/Getty Images

33 touchdowns to finish among the NFL's leading passers. After passing for a league-leading 4,267 yards in 2003, he shared the league's Most Valuable Player (MVP) award with Steve McNair of the Tennessee Titans. Manning won the MVP honour outright in 2004 with a sensational performance that included 49 touchdown passes and a passer rating of 121.1, both NFL records for a single season. (His touchdown record has since been broken.)

During the 2005 season, Manning led the Colts to victories in their first 13 games. Although considered one of the favourites to win the Super Bowl, the team lost in its opening postseason game. Manning's ability to win a championship was questioned by some observers, but in the 2006 season he silenced his critics. He threw for 4,397 yards—the seventh time in his career he had passed for more than 4,000 yards, breaking an NFL record—to lead the Colts to 12 wins during the regular season and a victory over the Chicago Bears in Super Bowl XLI. For his Super Bowl performance, which included 25 completed passes for 247 yards, Manning was named the game's MVP. In 2008 he won the league MVP award a third time, and in 2009 he led the Colts to a franchise-best 14–0 start to the season to earn a record fourth MVP award. While Manning helped the Colts to another Super Bowl berth the following February, the spectre of his past failure to win big games was again raised, as he threw a game-changing interception in the fourth quarter of a loss to the New Orleans Saints.

RANDY MOSS

(b. Feb. 13, 1977, Rand, W. Va., U.S.)

Randy Moss is considered one of the greatest wide receivers in NFL history.

Moss was a standout high school football and basketball player, but an arrest for battery during his senior year led the University of Notre Dame to withdraw its scholarship offer. He enrolled at Florida State University, but was kicked off the school's football team when he violated his parole by failing a drug test. With no more options to play for an upper-division college football program, he accepted a scholarship to Division I-AA (now called the Football Championship Subdivision) Marshall University. He set a number of I-AA receiving records in his freshman season while helping Marshall win a national championship. During his sophomore year, Marshall moved up to Division I-A (now the Football Bowl Subdivision), and Moss set a I-A record by catching 25 touchdown passes. Although Moss was widely considered to be one of the elite prospects in the 1998 NFL draft, he was not selected until the 21st pick of the first round (by the Minnesota Vikings), because of concerns about his character.

Moss took the league by storm in his first year with the Vikings. The mix of incredible speed, a rangy 6-foot 4-inch (1.93-metre) frame, and outstanding leaping ability—which had made Moss a difficult matchup in high school and college and earned him the nickname "The Freak" at Marshall—continued to befuddle defenders at football's highest level. His 17 receiving touchdowns in 1998 were a rookie record, resulting in his being named NFL Offensive Rookie of the Year and earning first-team All-Pro honours. Minnesota scored the most points in NFL history that season and posted a 15–1 record before losing in the NFC championship game. Moss amassed at least 14,000 receiving yards and caught 11 touchdown passes in each of the following two seasons, and he set career highs with 111 receptions for 1,632 yards in the 2003 regular season.

In 2005 the Vikings traded Moss to the Oakland Raiders. His two years in Oakland were relatively unproductive: Moss scored only 11 total touchdowns in his two seasons with the Raiders, and he was traded to the New England Patriots for a fourth-round draft pick in 2007.

Moss quickly turned his career around in New England. In the 2007 regular season he teamed with quarterback Tom Brady to form the core of a high-powered offense that broke the Vikings' single-season scoring mark while posting the first 16–0 regular-season record in NFL history. In addition, Moss caught 23 touchdown passes to break Jerry Rice's 20-year-old NFL record. However, the Patriots' storybook run ended with an upset loss to the New York Giants in the Super Bowl. In 2009 Moss caught his 141st career touchdown pass, the second highest total in NFL history behind Rice.

Four games into the 2010 season, Moss—who was in the last year of his contract and had publicly stated that he believed he was playing his final year in New England—was traded to the Vikings. His second stint in Minnesota lasted just four games, which were marked by nondescript on-field production and public questioning of his effort. He was waived by the Vikings and then claimed by the Tennessee Titans.

BILL PARCELLS

(b. Aug. 22, 1941, Englewood, N.J., U.S.)

Football coach and executive Bill Parcells coached the New York Giants to Super Bowl victories in 1987 and 1991.

Duane Charles Parcells spent most of his childhood in New Jersey, where he acquired the nickname "Bill" from teachers who confused him with another student. In high school Parcells played football, basketball, and baseball. Parcells was offered athletic scholarships to several colleges in both baseball and football. He chose to play football at New York's Colgate University but was dissatisfied with the team there and transferred after one year to Wichita State University in Kansas. He had a solid college career as a linebacker and was chosen by the Detroit Lions during the seventh round of the NFL's 1964 draft. Parcells was cut during training camp, however, and immediately turned to coaching.

Over the next 15 years Parcells held assistant coaching positions at Hastings (Neb.) College, Wichita State, the United States Military Academy, Florida State University, Vanderbilt University, and Texas Tech University. He received his first head coaching job at the United States Air Force Academy in Colorado Springs, Colo., in 1978. Frustrated with the recruiting that comes with coaching a college team, he accepted an assistant coaching position in 1979 with the New York Giants. His family resisted moving, however, and Parcells soon quit the Giants and came back to Colorado to begin a real estate career. Sensing his unhappiness, his wife urged him to return to football, and in 1980 he became the linebackers coach for the New England Patriots. In 1981 Parcells returned to the Giants as defensive coordinator. When the team's head coach left at the end of 1982, Parcells was promoted to that position.

Parcells—who was also known as "The Tuna"—quickly developed the Giants into a powerhouse team. After the Giants posted a disappointing 3–12–1 record in his first year guiding the team, Parcells led them to play-off berths in 1984 and 1985. He gained a measure of notoriety in 1985, when he was doused with the contents of a Gatorade sports drink cooler after a victory, a celebration that soon became commonplace after significant wins at all levels of football—and was carried over to other sports. In 1986 the Giants won 14 of their 16 games and steamrolled through the play-offs to capture the first Super Bowl title in franchise history in January 1987, which was also the Giants' first league championship of any kind since 1956. After Parcells's Giants won another Super Bowl in 1991, he retired and then signed with NBC Sports to serve as an analyst for its football broadcasts.

Parcells did not leave the field for long, however. In 1993 he became head coach of a New England Patriots team that was coming off of a 2–14 season. He turned the franchise around and led the Patriots to a Super Bowl appearance opposite the Green Bay Packers at the end of the 1996 season. In so doing, he became the second coach in NFL history (after Don Shula) to take two different teams to the Super Bowl, though the Patriots lost to the Packers. An acrimonious relationship with Patriots ownership led to Parcells's departure soon after the Super Bowl. He then became head coach and general manager of the New York Jets, which he took from a 1–15 record the year before his arrival to a 12–4 mark and a berth in the conference championship game in his second season. He stopped coaching the team after the

1999 season and stayed on as general manager for one more year before retiring once more in 2000.

In 2003 Parcells was lured back into the sport to become head coach of the Dallas Cowboys. He again took a team that had double-digit losses in the season before he arrived and led it to the play-offs, this time in his first season with the franchise, as the Cowboys went 10–6 but lost in the first round of the postseason. After guiding the team to a cumulative 34–30 record over four seasons, he retired from coaching a final time in 2007. Parcells then took over the football operations for the Miami Dolphins, where he oversaw an improvement of 10 wins in his first year with the franchise, which tied the NFL record for the greatest win increase from the previous season. In 2010 he ceded control of the Dolphins' operations but stayed on with the team as a consultant.

JOE PATERNO

(b. Dec. 21, 1926, Brooklyn, N.Y., U.S.)

As head coach at Pennsylvania State University (1966–), Joe Paterno became one of the most successful coaches in the history of the sport.

Joseph Vincent Paterno served in the U.S. Army in the final year of World War II before accepting an athletic scholarship to Brown University, where he studied English literature and played quarterback for the football team. Upon graduation in 1950, he intended to enroll in law school but was lured away when his former coach at Brown, Charles "Rip" Engle, became head coach at Pennsylvania State University (Penn State). After 16 years as Engle's assistant, Paterno succeeded him in 1966.

"JoePa" made an immediate impact on the program, leading Penn State to consecutive undefeated seasons in

1968 and 1969. The team posted another undefeated season in 1973. However, Penn State was denied a national championship in each of these three seasons, as it failed to finish first in the final football writers' polls that determined the national champion at that time. Penn State won its first national championship of the Paterno era in 1982 and added another—as well as a fourth undefeated season—in 1986. Penn State started playing football in the Big Ten Conference in 1993, and it won a conference title the following year after Paterno guided the Nittany Lions to a record of 12 wins and 0 losses. In 2001 Paterno posted his 324th career win, surpassing the record for all-time major college coaching victories held by Bear Bryant of the University of Alabama. (Paterno's victory tally was bested by Florida State's Bobby Bowden in 2003, and the two coaches remained in a close race for the record before both Bowden's retirement and Florida State's forfeited wins in 2010 gave Paterno the career victory record.) Paterno also owned the record for career coaching victories in bowl games.

In January 2002 Paterno became the first active coach in 20 years to receive the Amos Alonzo Stagg Award, the highest honour given by the American Football Coaches Association. A four-time winner of the association's Coach of the Year award, he was inducted into the College Football Hall of Fame in 2007. Not content only to build the football program, Paterno was an advocate for academic integrity and donated millions to build up the nonsporting programs of the university.

EDDIE ROBINSON

(b. Feb. 13, 1919, Jackson, La., U.S.—d. April 3, 2007, Ruston, La.)

Eddie Robinson was a collegiate football coach who set a record (later surpassed) for most career wins (408). He spent his entire head-coach career at Grambling State University in Louisiana. On Oct. 7, 1995, having guided Grambling to a 42–6 win over Mississippi Valley State, he became the first coach to claim 400 victories.

Edward Gay Robinson attended Leland College in Baker, La., where he played quarterback and led the team to a combined 18–1 record over the 1939 and 1940 seasons. During his final two years at Leland, he also served as an assistant coach. He earned his bachelor's degree in 1941 and received a master's degree from the University of Iowa in 1954.

In 1941 Grambling (then known as Louisiana Negro Normal and Industrial Institute) hired Robinson to coach football and basketball and teach physical education. In his first season he had no assistants and no budget for replacing equipment. He handled virtually everything himself, from mowing the field to taping players' ankles to writing accounts of the games for the local newspaper. That season his team posted a record of 3–5. The next season, however, he guided the team to a perfect 8–0 record.

Robinson's Grambling Tigers went on to have two more perfect seasons, capture 17 conference titles, and win several National Negro championships. In the 1960s, after several decades when football at historically black colleges went largely unnoticed by most football fans, Robinson's Grambling teams gained fame for sending more players into professional football than any school except Notre Dame. Among the more than 200 of his players who went on to compete in the National Football League were Hall of Fame members Willie Davis, Willie Brown, and Buck Buchanan. The racial integration of college football in the South in the 1970s ended this brief period of football glory for Grambling and other black colleges.

Surpassing Bear Bryant's record for wins, Robinson earned his 324th career victory on Oct. 5, 1985, with a 27–7 defeat of Prairie View A&M in Dallas. At the end of the 1997 season, he retired with a lifetime record of 408–165–15. Robinson's record of 408 career victories stood until 2003, when it was broken by John Gagliardi, coach of St. John's of Minnesota. The recipient of numerous awards, Robinson was inducted into the College Football Hall of Fame in 1997.

KNUTE ROCKNE

(b. March 4, 1888, Voss, Nor.—d. March 31, 1931, Chase County, Kan., U.S.)

Norwegian-born football coach Knute Rockne built the University of Notre Dame into a major power in college football and became the intercollegiate sport's first true celebrity coach.

In 1893 Rockne moved to Chicago with his family, and in 1910 he entered Notre Dame, where he played end on the football team and was also a track star. The 1913 game with Army, in which passes from Charles "Gus" Dorais to Rockne led to an upset victory by Notre Dame, is generally credited with popularizing the forward pass, legal since 1906 but not yet widely adopted. Following his graduation in 1914, Rockne taught chemistry and served as assistant football coach at Notre Dame under Jess Harper, becoming head coach in 1918 as well as athletic director.

Under Rockne, Notre Dame teams won 105 games, lost 12, and tied 5 from 1918 through 1931 and were declared national champions in 1924, 1929, and 1930 (there was no official poll in these years). Rockne's most famous player was George Gipp, a devil-may-care star who died in 1920 at the end of his senior season. Following Notre Dame's upset of Army in 1928, sportswriters spread the story that Rockne had inspired his players at halftime to "win one for the Gipper," a request the dying Gipp supposedly

whispered to Rockne. However, it was Rockne's undefeated 1924 team, featuring the Four Horsemen backfield
of star players, that marked Notre Dame's arrival at the
pinnacle of intercollegiate football, where it remained
under Rockne's many successors.

Notre Dame gained national recognition not just
through the excellence of its teams but also through
Rockne's tireless promoting and cultivation of prominent
sportswriters. Rockne gave his name to a ghostwritten syn-
dicated newspaper column and numerous magazine articles,
was a celebrated off-season banquet speaker, and became a
spokesman for several businesses and products, most conspicuously Studebaker automobiles, whose "Rockne" model
appeared just after he died. Rockne's death in a plane crash
in a Kansas cornfield in March 1931 shocked the nation and
prompted tributes from President Herbert Hoover and the
king of Norway. An outpouring of popular biographies and
testimonials to Rockne's genius, culminating in the 1940
film, *Knute Rockne—All-American* (with Ronald Reagan playing George Gipp), guaranteed his immortality as the most
famous of American football coaches.

MICHAEL STRAHAN

(b. Nov. 21, 1971, Houston, Texas, U.S.)

Playing defensive end for the New York Giants, Michael
Strahan established himself as one of the premier pass
rushers in the history of the NFL.

At age nine Strahan moved to Germany when his father,
a major in the U.S. Army, was stationed there. As a result, the
young Strahan played very little organized football growing up. An ardent weightlifter, he became strong enough
that his father believed he could earn a college football
scholarship, so Strahan was sent to live with his uncle—a

former NFL player—in Houston before his senior year of high school. He played well enough to obtain a scholarship to Texas Southern University, which competed in lower-division college football. Strahan set a school record with 41.5 sacks in his four years at Texas Southern and was selected by the Giants in the 1993 NFL draft.

After the 2000 regular season, Strahan helped the Giants reach Super Bowl XXXV, which the team lost to the Baltimore Ravens. In 2001 he recorded 22.5 sacks, an NFL single-season record, and was named the NFL's Defensive Player of the Year. He again led the league in sacks in 2003, totaling 18.5 over the course of the season. Strahan and the Giants advanced to another Super Bowl in February 2008, where they upset the previously undefeated New England Patriots. He retired months after that surprise victory, ending his career with seven Pro Bowl selections and four first-team All-Pro honours.

The gregarious Strahan had long been a popular commercial spokesman, and his signature gap-toothed smile became well known to American television audiences. His profitable endorsement sideline career continued after his retirement, and he also acted on a number of television shows.

LADAINIAN TOMLINSON

(b. June 23, 1979, Rosebud, Texas, U.S.)

One of the most productive running backs in pro football history, Tomlinson set an NFL record in 2006 by rushing for 28 touchdowns in a single season.

Tomlinson attended high school in Waco, Texas. Despite earning second-team all-state honours in his senior season, he was mostly overlooked by the major college football programs. He chose to attend Texas Christian

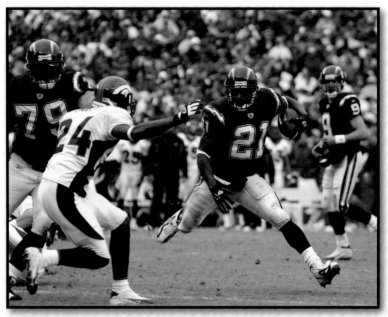

LaDanian Tomlinson (No. 21) had several outstanding years with the San Diego Chargers and began playing for the New York Jets in 2010. Donald Miralle/Getty Images

University (TCU) in nearby Fort Worth; he was the leading rusher in college football in his junior and senior years at the university.. Tomlinson finished fourth in Heisman Trophy balloting in 2000 and was selected by the San Diego Chargers with the fifth overall pick of the 2001 NFL draft.

Tomlinson was considered small for an NFL running back (5 feet 10 inches [1.77 metres] and about 220 pounds [100 kg]). He made up for his lack of size with a hard-nosed running style and terrific speed. A tremendous receiver, he was also one of the most versatile players in the game, adding more than 50 pass receptions to at least 1,200 rushing yards in each of his first seven seasons in the league. In 2003 Tomlinson became the only NFL player ever to rush for 1,000 yards and catch 100 passes in the same season, and he was one of only seven players in the history of the league to have run, caught, and passed for a touchdown in a single game.

In 2006 Tomlinson led the league in rushing yards and broke both Shaun Alexander's record for most touchdowns scored in one season (31) and the 46-year-old record for most single-season points scored (186). Tomlinson had reached another milestone earlier that season when he scored the 100th touchdown of his NFL career, accomplishing the feat in just 89 games—faster than anyone else in league history. His record-setting year resulted in him winning the NFL Most Valuable Player award for the 2006 season. Tomlinson helped propel the Chargers to a 14–2 record in 2006—the best in the NFL—but they were upset in their first play-off game by the New England Patriots. Tomlinson led the NFL in rushing yards and rushing touchdowns again in the 2007 season, which he followed by leading the Chargers to an AFC championship game loss in January 2008. His numbers declined over the following two seasons—in 2009 he rushed for a career-low 730 yards—and in 2010 he was released by San Diego and signed by the New York Jets.

EPILOGUE

Gridiron football has undergone a sea change since it was first played in the late 19th century. What was once a plodding, low-scoring sport almost indistinguishable from rugby has become an action-packed game that emphasizes the forward pass and features some of the most gifted athletes in the world. The public's perception of football also has drastically altered over time. The sport has transformed from a seemingly uncivilized and nearly illegal curiosity to the unquestioned king of U.S. spectator sports. The game is no longer considered merely a spectacle that appeals to fans' baser desires—as it was in its early years—but has arguably surpassed baseball to become the country's true national pastime.

APPENDIX: FOOTBALL CHAMPIONSHIP WINNERS

SUPER BOWL RESULTS

SUPER BOWL*					
	SEASON	RESULT			
I	1966–67	Green Bay Packers (NFL)	35	Kansas City Chiefs (AFL)	10
II	1967–68	Green Bay Packers (NFL)	33	Oakland Raiders (AFL)	14
III	1968–69	New York Jets (AFL)	16	Baltimore Colts (NFL)	7
IV	1969–70	Kansas City Chiefs (AFL)	23	Minnesota Vikings (NFL)	7
V	1970–71	Baltimore Colts (AFC)	16	Dallas Cowboys (NFC)	13
VI	1971–72	Dallas Cowboys (NFC)	24	Miami Dolphins (AFC)	3
VII	1972–73	Miami Dolphins (AFC)	14	Washington Redskins (NFC)	7
VIII	1973–74	Miami Dolphins (AFC)	24	Minnesota Vikings (NFC)	7
IX	1974–75	Pittsburgh Steelers (AFC)	16	Minnesota Vikings (NFC)	6
X	1975–76	Pittsburgh Steelers (AFC)	21	Dallas Cowboys (NFC)	17

	SEASON	RESULT			
XI	1976–77	Oakland Raiders (AFC)	32	Minnesota Vikings (NFC)	14
XII	1977–78	Dallas Cowboys (NFC)	27	Denver Broncos (AFC)	10
XIII	1978–79	Pittsburgh Steelers (AFC)	35	Dallas Cowboys (NFC)	31
XIV	1979–80	Pittsburgh Steelers (AFC)	31	Los Angeles Rams (NFC)	19
XV	1980–81	Oakland Raiders (AFC)	27	Philadelphia Eagles (NFC)	10
XVI	1981–82	San Francisco 49ers (NFC)	26	Cincinnati Bengals (AFC)	21
XVII	1982–83	Washington Redskins (NFC)	27	Miami Dolphins (AFC)	17
XVIII	1983–84	Los Angeles Raiders (AFC)	38	Washington Redskins (NFC)	9
XIX	1984–85	San Francisco 49ers (NFC)	38	Miami Dolphins (AFC)	16
XX	1985–86	Chicago Bears (NFC)	46	New England Patriots (AFC)	10
XXI	1986–87	New York Giants (NFC)	39	Denver Broncos (AFC)	20
XXII	1987–88	Washington Redskins (NFC)	42	Denver Broncos (AFC)	10
XXIII	1988–89	San Francisco 49ers (NFC)	20	Cincinnati Bengals (AFC)	16
XXIV	1989–90	San Francisco 49ers (NFC)	55	Denver Broncos (AFC)	10
XXV	1990–91	New York Giants (NFC)	20	Buffalo Bills (AFC)	19
XXVI	1991–92	Washington Redskins (NFC)	37	Buffalo Bills (AFC)	24

	SEASON	RESULT			
XXVII	1992–93	Dallas Cowboys (NFC)	52	Buffalo Bills (AFC)	17
XXVIII	1993–94	Dallas Cowboys (NFC)	30	Buffalo Bills (AFC)	13
XXIX	1994–95	San Francisco 49ers (NFC)	49	San Diego Chargers (AFC)	26
XXX	1995–96	Dallas Cowboys (NFC)	27	Pittsburgh Steelers (AFC)	17
XXXI	1996–97	Green Bay Packers (NFC)	35	New England Patriots (AFC)	21
XXXII	1997–98	Denver Broncos (AFC)	31	Green Bay Packers (NFC)	24
XXXIII	1998–99	Denver Broncos (AFC)	34	Atlanta Falcons (NFC)	19
XXXIV	1999–2000	St. Louis Rams (NFC)	23	Tennessee Titans (AFC)	16
XXXV	2000–01	Baltimore Ravens (AFC)	34	New York Giants (NFC)	7
XXXVI	2001–02	New England Patriots (AFC)	20	St. Louis Rams (NFC)	17
XXXVII	2002–03	Tampa Bay Buccaneers (NFC)	48	Oakland Raiders (AFC)	21
XXXVIII	2003–04	New England Patriots (AFC)	32	Carolina Panthers (NFC)	29
XXXIX	2004–05	New England Patriots (AFC)	24	Philadelphia Eagles (NFC)	21
XL	2005–06	Pittsburgh Steelers (AFC)	21	Seattle Seahawks (NFC)	10
XLI	2006–07	Indianapolis Colts (AFC)	29	Chicago Bears (NFC)	17

	SEASON	RESULT			
XLII	2007–08	New York Giants (NFC)	17	New England Patriots (AFC)	14
XLIII	2008–09	Pittsburgh Steelers (AFC)	27	Arizona Cardinals (NFC)	23
XLIV	2009–10	New Orleans Saints (NFC)	31	Indianapolis Colts (AFC)	17
XLV	2010-11	Green Bay Packers (NFC)	31	Pittsburgh Steelers (AFC)	25

*NFL-AFL championship 1966–70; NFL championship from 1970–71 season.

COLLEGE FOOTBALL NATIONAL CHAMPIONS

COLLEGE FOOTBALL NATIONAL CHAMPIONS*	
SEASON	CHAMPION
1924	Notre Dame
1925	Dartmouth
1926	Stanford
1927	Illinois
1928	Southern California
1929	Notre Dame
1930	Notre Dame
1931	Southern California
1932	Michigan
1933	Michigan
1934	Minnesota
1935	Southern Methodist
1936	Minnesota
1937	Pittsburgh
1938	Texas Christian

SEASON	CHAMPION
1939	Texas A&M
1940	Minnesota
1941	Minnesota
1942	Ohio State
1943	Notre Dame
1944	Army
1945	Army
1946	Notre Dame
1947	Notre Dame
1948	Michigan
1949	Notre Dame
1950	Oklahoma
1951	Tennessee
1952	Michigan State
1953	Maryland
1954	Ohio State (AP), UCLA (UP)
1955	Oklahoma
1956	Oklahoma
1957	Auburn (AP), Ohio State (UP)
1958	Louisiana State
1959	Syracuse
1960	Minnesota
1961	Alabama
1962	Southern California
1963	Texas
1964	Alabama
1965	Alabama (AP), Michigan State (UPI)
1966	Notre Dame
1967	Southern California

SEASON	CHAMPION
1968	Ohio State
1969	Texas
1970	Nebraska (AP), Texas (UPI)
1971	Nebraska
1972	Southern California
1973	Notre Dame (AP), Alabama (UPI)
1974	Oklahoma (AP), Southern California (UPI)
1975	Oklahoma
1976	Pittsburgh
1977	Notre Dame
1978	Alabama (AP), Southern California (UPI)
1979	Alabama
1980	Georgia
1981	Clemson
1982	Penn State
1983	Miami (Fla.)
1984	Brigham Young
1985	Oklahoma
1986	Penn State
1987	Miami (Fla.)
1988	Notre Dame
1989	Miami (Fla.)
1990	Colorado (AP), Georgia Tech (UPI)
1991	Miami (Fla.; AP), Washington (UPI)
1992	Alabama
1993	Florida State
1994	Nebraska
1995	Nebraska
1996	Florida

SEASON	CHAMPION
1997	Michigan (AP), Nebraska (USA Today/ESPN)
1998	Tennessee
1999	Florida State
2000	Oklahoma
2001	Miami (Fla.)
2002	Ohio State
2003	Louisiana State (BCS), Southern California (AP)
2004	Southern California
2005	Texas
2006	Florida
2007	Louisiana State
2008	Florida
2009	Alabama
2010	Auburn

*National champion determined by various polls until the introduction of the BCS system in 1998.

GREY CUP RESULTS

GREY CUP	
YEAR	RESULT
1909	U. of Toronto
1910	U. of Toronto
1911	U. of Toronto
1912	Hamilton Alerts
1913	Hamilton Tigers
1914	Toronto Argonauts
1915	Hamilton Tigers
1916–19	No competition
1920	U. of Toronto
1921*	Toronto Argonauts

YEAR	RESULT			
1922	Queen's University	13	Edmonton Eskimos	1
1923	Queen's University	54	Regina Roughriders	0
1924	Queen's University	11	Toronto Balmy Beach	3
1925	Ottawa Rough Riders	24	Winnipeg Blue Bombers	1
1926	Ottawa Rough Riders	10	U. of Toronto	7
1927	Toronto Balmy Beach	9	Hamilton Tigers	6
1928	Hamilton Tigers	30	Regina Roughriders	0
1929	Hamilton Tigers	14	Regina Roughriders	3
1930	Toronto Balmy Beach	11	Regina Roughriders	6
1931	Montreal AAA	22	Regina Roughriders	0
1932	Hamilton Tigers	25	Regina Roughriders	6
1933	Toronto Argonauts	4	Sarnia Imperials	3
1934	Sarnia Imperials	20	Regina Roughriders	12
1935	Winnipeg Blue Bombers	18	Hamilton Tigers	12
1936	Sarnia Imperials	26	Ottawa Rough Riders	20
1937	Toronto Argonauts	4	Winnipeg Blue Bombers	3
1938	Toronto Argonauts	30	Winnipeg Blue Bombers	7
1939	Winnipeg Blue Bombers	8	Ottawa Rough Riders	7
1940	Ottawa Rough Riders	**	Toronto Balmy Beach	**
1941	Winnipeg Blue Bombers	18	Ottawa Rough Riders	16
1942	Toronto RCAF Hurricanes	8	Winnipeg Blue Bombers	5
1943	Hamilton Flying Wildcats	23	Winnipeg Blue Bombers	14
1944	Montreal S. Hyacinthe-Donnaconna	7	Hamilton Wildcats	6
1945	Toronto Argonauts	35	Winnipeg Blue Bombers	0
1946	Toronto Argonauts	28	Winnipeg Blue Bombers	0
1947	Toronto Argonauts	10	Winnipeg Blue Bombers	9

YEAR	RESULT			
1948	Calgary Stampeders	12	Ottawa Rough Riders	7
1949	Montreal Alouettes	28	Calgary Stampeders	15
1950	Toronto Argonauts	13	Winnipeg Blue Bombers	0
1951	Ottawa Rough Riders	21	Saskatchewan Roughriders	14
1952	Toronto Argonauts	21	Edmonton Eskimos	11
1953	Hamilton Tiger-Cats	12	Winnipeg Blue Bombers	6
1954	Edmonton Eskimos	26	Montreal Alouettes	25
1955	Edmonton Eskimos	34	Montreal Alouettes	19
1956	Edmonton Eskimos	50	Montreal Alouettes	27
1957	Hamilton Tiger-Cats	32	Winnipeg Blue Bombers	7
1958	Winnipeg Blue Bombers	35	Hamilton Tiger-Cats	28
1959	Winnipeg Blue Bombers (WFC)	21	Hamilton Tiger-Cats (EFC)	7
1960	Ottawa Rough Riders (EFC)	16	Edmonton Eskimos (WFC)	6
1961	Winnipeg Blue Bombers (WFC)	21	Hamilton Tiger-Cats (EFC)	14
1962	Winnipeg Blue Bombers (WFC)	28	Hamilton Tiger-Cats (EFC)	27
1963	Hamilton Tiger-Cats (EFC)	21	British Columbia Lions (WFC)	10
1964	British Columbia Lions (WFC)	34	Hamilton Tiger-Cats (EFC)	24
1965	Hamilton Tiger-Cats (EFC)	22	Winnipeg Blue Bombers (WFC)	16
1966	Saskatchewan Roughriders (WFC)	29	Ottawa Rough Riders (EFC)	14
1967	Hamilton Tiger-Cats (EFC)	24	Saskatchewan Roughriders (WFC)	1

YEAR	RESULT			
1968	Ottawa Rough Riders (EFC)	24	Calgary Stampeders (WFC)	21
1969	Ottawa Rough Riders (EFC)	29	Saskatchewan Roughriders (WFC)	11
1970	Montreal Alouettes (EFC)	23	Calgary Stampeders (WFC)	10
1971	Calgary Stampeders (WFC)	14	Toronto Argonauts (EFC)	11
1972	Hamilton Tiger-Cats (EFC)	13	Saskatchewan Roughriders (WFC)	10
1973	Ottawa Rough Riders (EFC)	22	Edmonton Eskimos (WFC)	18
1974	Montreal Alouettes (EFC)	20	Edmonton Eskimos (WFC)	7
1975	Edmonton Eskimos (WFC)	9	Montreal Alouettes (EFC)	8
1976	Ottawa Rough Riders (EFC)	23	Saskatchewan Roughriders (WFC)	20
1977	Montreal Alouettes (EFC)	41	Edmonton Eskimos (WFC)	6
1978	Edmonton Eskimos (WFC)	20	Montreal Alouettes (EFC)	13
1979	Edmonton Eskimos (WFC)	17	Montreal Alouettes (EFC)	9
1980	Edmonton Eskimos (WFC)	48	Hamilton Tiger-Cats (EFC)	10
1981	Edmonton Eskimos (WFC)	26	Ottawa Rough Riders (EFC)	23
1982	Edmonton Eskimos (WFC)	32	Toronto Argonauts (EFC)	16
1983	Toronto Argonauts (EFC)	18	British Columbia Lions (WFC)	17

YEAR	RESULT			
1984	Winnipeg Blue Bombers (WFC)	47	Hamilton Tiger-Cats (EFC)	17
1985	British Columbia Lions (WFC)	37	Hamilton Tiger-Cats (EFC)	24
1986	Hamilton Tiger-Cats (EFC)	39	Edmonton Eskimos (WFC)	15
1987	Edmonton Eskimos (WFC)	38	Toronto Argonauts (EFC)	36
1988	Winnipeg Blue Bombers (EFC)	22	British Columbia Lions (WFC)	21
1989	Saskatchewan Roughriders (WFC)	43	Hamilton Tiger-Cats (EFC)	40
1990	Winnipeg Blue Bombers (EFC)	50	Edmonton Eskimos (WFC)	11
1991	Toronto Argonauts (EFC)	36	Calgary Stampeders (WFC)	21
1992	Calgary Stampeders (WFC)	24	Winnipeg Blue Bombers (EFC)	10
1993	Edmonton Eskimos (WFC)	33	Winnipeg Blue Bombers (EFC)	23
1994	British Columbia Lions (WFC)	26	Baltimore Stallions (EFC)	23
1995	Baltimore Stallions (SD)	37	Calgary Stampeders (ND)	20
1996	Toronto Argonauts (ED)	43	Edmonton Eskimos (WD)	37
1997	Toronto Argonauts (ED)	47	Saskatchewan Roughriders (WD)	23
1998	Calgary Stampeders (WD)	26	Hamilton Tiger-Cats (ED)	24
1999	Hamilton Tiger-Cats (ED)	32	Calgary Stampeders (WD)	21

YEAR	RESULT			
2000	British Columbia Lions (WD)	28	Montreal Alouettes (ED)	26
2001	Calgary Stampeders (WD)	27	Winnipeg Blue Bombers (ED)	19
2002	Montreal Alouettes (ED)	25	Edmonton Eskimos (WD)	16
2003	Edmonton Eskimos (WD)	34	Montreal Alouettes (ED)	22
2004	Toronto Argonauts (ED)	27	British Columbia Lions (WD)	19
2005	Edmonton Eskimos (WD)	38	Montreal Alouettes (ED)	35
2006	British Columbia Lions (WD)	25	Montreal Alouettes (ED)	14
2007	Saskatchewan Roughriders (WD)	23	Winnipeg Blue Bombers (ED)	19
2008	Calgary Stampeders (WD)	22	Montreal Alouettes (ED)	14
2009	Montreal Alouettes (ED)	28	Saskatchewan Roughriders (WD)	27
2010	Montreal Alouettes (ED)	21	Saskatchewan Roughriders (WD)	18

*East-West playoff began in 1921.
**Ottawa won the two-game total-point series 8–2 and 12–5.

GLOSSARY

blitz A rush of the passer by a defensive linebacker or back.

booster In collegiate athletics, a person (typically an alumnus of the school) who supports a team or athletic program, often financially.

conversion A successful attempt for a point or points after a touchdown or for a first down.

cornerback A defensive back positioned on the outside flank or "corner" of the defensive line.

down A play from scrimmage during which an offense attempts to advance the ball against a defense.

field goal A score of three points, made by kicking the ball over the crossbar and between the goal posts from ordinary play.

free agent A professional athlete whose contract or commitment to a specific team has ended, leaving him or her free to negotiate with other teams.

fumble To lose control of the football after establishing possession of it.

"gentleman's agreement" An unofficial agreement among National Football League owners that kept African Americans out of the league between 1934 and 1945.

gridiron Football field, so named for the vertical yard lines marking the rectangular field.

hash mark The lines on a football field that mark one-yard increments.

huddle A gathering of football players, away from the line of scrimmage, that typically occurs before each play so that players can receive instructions for the upcoming down.

linemen Football players in the forward line of an offense or defense.

pocket On a passing down, the area behind the line of scrimmage and between the offensive tackles that allows the quarterback room to move and time to throw the ball.

punt To drop-kick the ball to the opposing side, which usually occurs on fourth down.

sack Tackling the quarterback behind the line of scrimmage

safety A situation in which a member of the offense is downed behind his own goal line, which results in two points and possession of the ball for the opposing team.

scrimmage The possession of the football by one side for a determined period of time, as opposed to a scrummage (an older form of possession in gridiron football) in which teams continually alternate possessions. The imaginary line that is established by the position of the ball before a play is known as the "line of scrimmage."

shotgun formation An offensive formation in which the quarterback stands a few yards behind the centre, as opposed to directly behind the centre, before the ball is snapped to him.

spotting In football, placing the ball at a specific spot where play has ended.

tackle To stop the forward progress of a ballcarrier by bringing him to the ground.

wing Also known as a wingback; a player who is positioned either behind or flanking an end of an offensive line; antiquated position.

BIBLIOGRAPHY

The most comprehensive history of the U.S. intercollegiate game is John Sayle Watterson, *College Football: History, Spectacle, Controversy* (2000). Michael Oriard, *Reading Football: How the Popular Press Created an American Spectacle* (1993), and *King Football: Sport and Spectacle in the Golden Age of Radio & Newsreels, Movies & Magazines, the Weekly & the Daily Press* (2001); Murray Sperber, *Shake Down the Thunder: The Creation of Notre Dame Football* (1993, reissued 2002), and *Onward to Victory: The Crises That Shaped College Sports* (1998); David M. Nelson, *The Anatomy of a Game: Football, the Rules, and the Men Who Made the Game* (1994); and Robin Lester, *Stagg's University: The Rise, Decline, and Fall of Big-Time Football at Chicago* (1995), also are authoritative treatments of aspects of the game. The NCAA publishes useful annuals.

For U.S. professional football, the most authoritative source is Bob Carroll, Michael Gersham, David Neft, and John Thorn (eds.), *Total Football: The Official Encyclopedia of the National Football League*, rev. and updated ed. (1999; also published as *Total Football II*). Robert W. Peterson, *Pigskin: The Early Years of Pro Football* (1997), provides a narrative history of the NFL's pretelevision era. A comprehensive narrative history of the NFL through the first years of the 21st century is found in Michael MacCambridge, *America's Game: The Epic Story of How Pro Football Captured a Nation* (2004). Jeff Miller, *Going Long: The Wild Ten-Year Saga of the Renegade American Football*

League in the Words of Those Who Lived It (2003), is a standout history of the AFL. *The Sporting News Pro Football Guide* is published annually.

Elements of the U.S. professional game are colourfully explored in George Plimpton, *Paper Lion* (1966); Jerry Kramer and Dick Schaap, *Instant Replay: The Green Bay Diary of Jerry Kramer* (1968, reissued 2006); and Michael Lewis, *The Blind Side: Evolution of a Game* (2006). Racial aspects are documented in Arthur R. Ashe, Jr., *A Hard Road to Glory—Football: The African-American Athlete in Football* (1993); Michael Hurd, *Black College Football, 1892–1992: One Hundred Years of History, Education and Pride*, rev., expanded 2nd ed. (1998); and Charles K. Ross, *Outside the Lines: African Americans and the Integration of the National Football League* (1999).

A compelling account of the impact of high school football on a small Texas town is found in H.G. Bissinger, *Friday Night Lights: A Town, a Team, and a Dream* (1990).

The most reliable histories of Canadian football are Frank Cosentino, *Canadian Football: The Grey Cup Years* (1969), and *A Passing Game: A History of the CFL* (1995). Current information can be found in the Canadian Football League annual, *Facts, Figures and Records*.

INDEX

C

Calhoun, George, 72, 138
Camp, Walter, 2–6, 9, 16, 20, 22, 24, 25
Campbell, Earl, 119, 120
Canadian football, 1, 40–44, 46, 212
Canadian Football League (CFL), 42–44, 46, 212
Carolina Panthers, 78–79, 193
Carr, Joe, 21
Carter, Cris, 76
centres, 4, 17, 45–46, 111, 128, 141
Chicago Bears, 13, 20, 66–69, 140, 151, 157, 177
Cincinnati Bengals, 92, 104–106, 143, 176–177
Cleveland Browns, 50, 87, 106–110, 139, 143, 145–146, 174, 209
coaches
  college football, 5, 9, 16–19, 201–203, 207–208, 213, 222–226
  influence of, 16–19, 52, 53–54
  professional football, 25, 51, 66, 74, 84, 92, 100, 124, 136–138, 143–144, 146–148, 157–159, 163–164, 166–169, 174–176, 189–192, 220–222
Coaches' Poll, 32, 33, 34
College All-Star Game, 21
college football
  bowl games, 14–15, 31–34
  conferences, 8, 14–15, 24, 26, 28–29, 30, 32–33, 52
  creation of, 1–11
  golden age of, 11–19
  great players, 201–229
  racial transformation of, 23–27, 37
  revenues earned, 28–29, 31, 41
  rules, 2, 4–5, 6, 8, 10, 19, 37, 48, 50

College Football Hall of Fame, 5, 9, 14, 25, 153, 172, 203, 209, 213, 223, 225
Columbia University, 2, 140
commercialization, 31, 133
conferences
  college football, 8, 14–15, 24, 26, 28–29, 30, 32–33, 52
  professional football, 23, 27, 36, 42, 56, 57–94, 94–132
contracts, coaches', 31
contracts, television, 28, 29, 34, 35, 36
conversions, 46, 47
Cornell University, 2, 17
cornerbacks, 52, 54, 66, 77, 99, 112, 128, 149, 150, 164, 182, 199
Coryell, Don, 131
Cotton Bowl, 15, 26, 31, 32–33, 208
Csonka, Larry, 53, 61, 97, 98

D

Dallas Cowboys, 57–59, 157, 163, 171, 198, 222
Dallas Texans, 114, 125
Davis, Al, 127–129, 166–169, 191
Davis, Ernie, 108, 208–209
Dawg Pound, 108–110
defense, 46, 47, 52–54
defensive ends, 4, 9, 51, 59, 68, 83, 87, 88, 92, 96, 114, 127, 157, 159, 160, 194, 207, 225, 226
Defensive Player of the Year, NFL, 88, 178, 181, 193, 194, 200, 206, 216, 227
Defensive Rookie of the Year, NFL, 112, 181
Deland, Lorin, 16